INDIAN HEROES
AND
GREAT CHIEFTAINS

INDIAN HEROES
AND
GREAT CHIEFTAINS

Charles A. Eastman
(Ohiyesa)

DOVER PUBLICATIONS, INC.
Mineola, New York

Copyright

Published in Canada by General Publishing Company, Ltd., 30 Lesmill Road, Don Mills, Toronto, Ontario.
Published in the United Kingdom by Constable and Company, Ltd., 3 The Lanchesters, 162–164 Fulham Palace Road, London W6 9ER.

Bibliographical Note

This Dover edition, first published in 1997, is an unabridged republication of the text of the work originally published by Little, Brown and Company, Boston, 1918. The picture selection differs in the present edition.

Library of Congress Cataloging-in-Publication Data

Eastman, Charles Alexander, 1858–1939.
    Indian heroes and great chieftains / Charles A. Eastman (Ohiyesa).
      p.   cm.
    "This Dover edition, first published in 1997, is an unabridged republication of the text of the work originally published by Little, Brown and Company, Boston, 1918. The picture selection differs in the present edition"—T.p. verso.
    ISBN 0-486-29608-3 (pbk.)
    1. Indians of North America—Biography. 2. Dakota Indians—Biography. I. Title.
E89.E13   1997
970' .00497'00922—dc21
[B]   97-5514
                                        CIP

Manufactured in the United States of America
Dover Publications, Inc., 31 East 2nd Street, Mineola, N.Y. 11501

Contents

List of Portraits

The portraits follow page 58.

INDIAN HEROES
AND
GREAT CHIEFTAINS

Red Cloud

EVERY age, every race, has its leaders and heroes. There were over sixty distinct tribes of Indians on this continent, each of which boasted its notable men. The names and deeds of some of these men will live in American history, yet in the true sense they are unknown, because misunderstood. I should like to present some of the greatest chiefs of modern times in the light of the native character and ideals, believing that the American people will gladly do them tardy justice.

It is matter of history that the Sioux nation, to which I belong, was originally friendly to the Caucasian peoples which it met in succession—first, to the south the Spaniards; then the French, on the Mississippi River and along the Great Lakes; later the English, and finally the Americans. This powerful tribe then roamed over the whole extent of the Mississippi valley, between that river and the Rockies. Their usages and government united the various bands more closely than was the case with many of the neighboring tribes.

During the early part of the nineteenth century, chiefs such as Wabashaw, Redwing, and Little Six among the eastern Sioux, Conquering Bear, Man-Afraid-of-His-Horse, and Hump of the western bands, were the last of the old type. After these, we have a coterie of new leaders, products of the new conditions brought about by close contact with the conquering race.

This distinction must be borne in mind—that while the early chiefs were spokesmen and leaders in the simplest sense, possessing no real authority, those who headed their tribes during the transition period were more or less rulers and more or less politicians. It is a singular fact that many of the "chiefs", well known as such to the American public, were not chiefs at all according to the accepted usages of their tribesmen. Their prominence was simply the result of an abnormal situation, in which representatives of the United States Government made use of them for a definite purpose. In a few cases, where a chief met with a violent death, some ambitious man has taken advantage of the confusion to thrust himself upon the tribe and, perhaps with outside help, has succeeded in usurping the leadership.

Red Cloud was born about 1820 near the forks of the Platte River. He was one of a family of nine children whose father, an able and respected warrior, reared his son under the old Spartan régime. The young Red Cloud is said to have been a fine horseman, able to swim across the Missouri and Yellowstone rivers, of high bearing and unquestionable courage, yet invariably gentle and courteous in everyday life. This last trait, together with a singularly musical and agreeable voice, has always been characteristic of the man.

When he was about six years old, his father gave him a spirited colt, and said to him:

"My son, when you are able to sit quietly upon the back of this colt without saddle or bridle, I shall be glad, for the boy who can win a wild creature and learn to use it will as a man be able to win and rule men."

The little fellow, instead of going for advice and help to his grandfather, as most Indian boys would have done, began quietly to practice throwing the lariat. In a little while he was able to lasso the colt. He was dragged off his feet at once, but hung on, and finally managed to picket him near the teepee. When the big boys drove the herd of ponies to water, he drove his colt with the rest. Presently the pony became used to him and allowed himself to be handled. The boy began to ride him bareback; he was thrown many times, but persisted until he could ride without even a lariat, sitting with arms folded and guiding the animal by the movements of his body. From that time on he told me that he broke all his own ponies, and before long his father's as well.

The old men, his contemporaries, have often related to me how Red Cloud was always successful in the hunt because his horses were so well broken. At the age of nine, he began to ride his father's pack pony upon the buffalo hunt. He was twelve years old, he told me, when he was first permitted to take part in the chase, and found to his great mortification that none of his arrows penetrated more than a few inches. Excited to recklessness, he whipped his horse nearer the fleeing buffalo, and before his father knew what he was about, he had seized one of the protruding arrows and tried to push it deeper. The furious animal tossed his massive head sidewise, and boy and horse were whirled into the air. Fortunately, the boy was thrown on the farther side of his pony, which received the full force of the second attack. The thundering hoofs of the stampeded herd soon passed them by, but the wounded and maddened buffalo refused to move, and some critical moments passed before Red Cloud's father succeeded in attracting its attention so that the boy might spring to his feet and run for his life.

I once asked Red Cloud if he could recall having ever been afraid, and in reply he told me this story. He was about sixteen years old and had already been once or twice upon the warpath, when one fall his people were hunting in the Big Horn country, where they might expect trouble at any moment with the hostile Crows or Shoshones. Red Cloud had followed a single buffalo bull into the Bad Lands and was out of sight and hearing of his companions. When he had brought down his game, he noted carefully every feature of his surroundings so that he might at once detect anything unusual, and tied his horse with a long lariat to the horn of the dead bison, while skinning and cutting up the meat so as to pack it to camp. Every few minutes he paused in his work to scrutinize the landscape, for he had a feeling that danger was not far off.

Suddenly, almost over his head, as it seemed, he heard a tremendous war whoop, and glancing sidewise, thought he beheld the charge of an overwhelming number of warriors. He tried desperately to give the usual undaunted war whoop in reply, but instead a yell of terror burst from his lips, his legs gave way under him, and he fell in a heap. When he realized, the next instant, that the war whoop was merely the sudden loud whinnying of his own horse, and the charging army a band of fleeing elk, he was so ashamed of himself that he never forgot the incident, although up to that time he had never mentioned it. His subsequent career would indicate that the lesson was well learned.

The future leader was still a very young man when he joined a war party against the Utes. Having pushed eagerly forward on the trail, he found himself far in advance of his companions as night came on, and at the same time rain began to fall heavily. Among the scattered scrub pines, the lone warrior found a natural cave, and after a hasty examination, he decided to shelter there for the night.

Scarcely had he rolled himself in his blanket when he heard a slight rustling at the entrance, as if some creature were preparing to share his retreat. It was pitch dark. He could see nothing, but judged that it must be either a man or a grizzly. There was not room to draw a bow. It must be between knife and knife, or between knife and claws, he said to himself.

The intruder made no search but quietly lay down in the opposite corner of the cave. Red Cloud remained perfectly still, scarcely breathing, his hand upon his knife. Hour after hour he lay broad awake, while many thoughts passed through his brain. Suddenly, without warning, he sneezed, and instantly a strong man sprang to a sitting posture opposite. The first gray of morning was creeping into their rocky den, and behold! a Ute hunter sat before him.

Desperate as the situation appeared, it was not without a grim humor. Neither could afford to take his eyes from the other's; the tension was great, till at last a smile wavered over the expressionless face of the Ute. Red Cloud answered the smile, and in that instant a treaty of peace was born between them.

"Put your knife in its sheath. I shall do so also, and we will smoke together," signed Red Cloud. The other assented gladly, and they ratified thus the truce which assured to each a safe return to his friends. Having finished their smoke, they shook hands and separated. Neither had given the other any information. Red Cloud returned to his party and told his story, adding that he had divulged nothing and had nothing to report. Some were inclined to censure him for not fighting, but he was sustained by a majority of the warriors, who commended his self-restraint. In a day or two they discovered the main camp of the enemy and fought a remarkable battle, in which Red Cloud especially distinguished himself.

The Sioux were now entering upon the most stormy period of their history. The old things were fast giving place to new. The young men, for the first time engaging in serious and destructive warfare with the neighboring tribes, armed with the deadly weapons furnished by the white man, began to realize that they must soon enter upon a desperate struggle for their ancestral hunting grounds. The old men had been innocently cultivating the friendship of the stranger, saying among themselves, "Surely there is land enough for all!"

Red Cloud was a modest and little known man of about twenty-eight years, when General Harney called all the western bands of Sioux together at Fort Laramie, Wyoming, for the purpose of securing an agreement and right of way through their territory. The Ogallalas held aloof from this proposal, but Bear Bull, an Ogallala chief, after having been plied with whisky, undertook to dictate submission to the rest of the clan. Enraged by failure, he fired upon a group of his own tribesmen, and Red Cloud's father and brother fell dead. According to Indian custom, it fell to him to avenge the deed. Calmly, without uttering a word, he faced old Bear Bull and his son, who attempted to defend his father, and shot them both. He did what he believed to be his duty, and the whole band sustained him. Indeed, the tragedy gave the young man at once a certain standing, as one who not only defended his people against enemies from without, but against injustice and aggression within the tribe. From this time on he was a recognized leader.

Man-Afraid-of-His-Horse, then head chief of the Ogallalas, took council with Red Cloud in all important matters, and the young warrior rapidly advanced in authority and influence. In 1854, when he was barely thirty-five years old, the various bands were again encamped near Fort Laramie. A Mormon emigrant train, moving westward, left a footsore cow behind, and the young men killed her for food. The next day, to their astonishment, an officer with thirty men appeared at the Indian camp and demanded of old Conquering Bear that they be given up.

The chief in vain protested that it was all a mistake and offered to make reparation. It would seem that either the officer was under the influence of liquor, or else had a mind to bully the Indians, for he would accept neither explanation nor payment, but demanded point-blank that the young men who had killed the cow be delivered up to summary punishment. The old chief refused to be intimidated and was shot dead on the spot. Not one soldier ever reached the gate of Fort Laramie! Here Red Cloud led the young Ogallalas, and so intense was the feeling that they even killed the half-breed interpreter.

Curiously enough, there was no attempt at retaliation on the part of the army, and no serious break until 1860, when the Sioux were involved in troubles with the Cheyennes and Arapahoes. In 1862, a grave outbreak was precipitated by the eastern Sioux in Minnesota under Little Crow, in which the western bands took no part. Yet this event ushered in a new period for their race. The surveyors of the Union Pacific were laying out the proposed road through the heart of the southern buffalo country, the rendezvous of Ogallalas, Brulés, Arapahoes, Comanches, and Pawnees, who followed the buffalo as a means of livelihood. To be sure, most of these tribes were at war with one another, yet during the summer months they met often to proclaim a truce and hold joint councils and festivities, which were now largely turned into discussions of the common enemy. It became evident, however, that some of the smaller and weaker tribes were inclined to welcome the new order of things, recognizing that it was the policy of the government to put an end to tribal warfare.

Red Cloud's position was uncompromisingly against submission. He made some noted speeches in this line, one of which was repeated to me by an old man who had heard and remembered it with the remarkable verbal memory of an Indian.

"Friends," said Red Cloud, "it has been our misfortune to welcome the white man. We have been deceived. He brought with him some shining things that pleased our eyes; he brought weapons more effective than our own: above all, he brought the spirit water that makes one forget for a time old age, weakness, and sorrow. But I wish to say to you that if you would possess these things for yourselves, you must begin anew and put away the wisdom of your fathers. You must lay up food, and forget the hungry. When your house is built, your storeroom filled, then look around for a neighbor whom you can take at a disadvantage, and seize all that he has! Give away only what you do not want; or rather, do not part with any of your possessions unless in exchange for another's.

"My countrymen, shall the glittering trinkets of this rich man, his deceitful drink that overcomes the mind, shall these things tempt us to give up our homes, our hunting grounds, and the honorable teaching of our old men? Shall we permit ourselves to be driven to and fro—to be herded like the cattle of the white man?"

His next speech that has been remembered was made in 1866, just before the attack on Fort Phil Kearny. The tension of feeling against the invaders had now reached its height. There was no dissenting voice in the council upon the Powder River, when it was decided to oppose to the uttermost the evident purpose of the government. Red Cloud was not altogether ignorant of the numerical strength and the resourcefulness of the white man, but he was determined to face any odds rather than submit.

"Hear ye, Dakotas!" he exclaimed. "When the Great Father at Washington sent us his chief soldier [General Harney] to ask for a path through our hunting grounds, a way for his iron road to the mountains and the western sea, we were told that they wished merely to pass through our country, not to tarry among us, but to seek for gold in the far west. Our old chiefs thought to show their friendship and good will, when they allowed this dangerous snake in our midst. They promised to protect the wayfarers.

"Yet before the ashes of the council fire are cold, the Great Father is building his forts among us. You have heard the sound of the white soldier's ax upon the Little Piney. His presence here is an insult and a threat. It is an insult to the spirits of our ancestors. Are we then to give up their sacred graves to be plowed for corn? Dakotas, I am for war!"

In less than a week after this speech, the Sioux advanced upon Fort Phil Kearny, the new sentinel that had just taken her place upon the farthest frontier, guarding the Oregon Trail. Every detail of the attack had been planned with care, though not without heated discussion, and nearly every well-known Sioux chief had agreed in striking the blow. The brilliant young war leader, Crazy Horse, was appointed to lead the charge. His lieutenants were Sword, Hump, and Dull Knife, with Little Chief of the Cheyennes, while the older men acted as councilors. Their success was instantaneous. In less than half an hour, they had cut down nearly a hundred men under Captain Fetterman, whom they drew out of the fort by a ruse and then annihilated.

Instead of sending troops to punish, the government sent a commission to treat with the Sioux. The result was the famous treaty of 1868, which Red Cloud was the last to sign, having refused to do so until all of the forts within their territory should be vacated. All of his demands were acceded to, the new road abandoned, the garrisons withdrawn, and in the new treaty it was distinctly stated that the Black Hills and the Big Horn were Indian country, set apart for their perpetual occupancy, and that no white man should enter that region without the consent of the Sioux.

Scarcely was this treaty signed, however, when gold was discovered in the Black Hills, and the popular cry was: "Remove the Indians!" This was easier said than done. That very territory had just been solemnly guaranteed to them forever: yet how stem the irresistible rush for gold? The government, at first, entered some small protest, just enough to "save its face", as the saying is; but there was no serious attempt to prevent the wholesale violation of the treaty. It was this state of affairs that led to the last great speech made by Red Cloud, at a gathering upon the Little Rosebud River. It is brief, and touches upon the hopelessness of their future as a race. He seems at about this time to have reached the conclusion that resistance could not last much longer; in fact, the greater part of the Sioux nation was already under government control.

"We are told," said he, "that Spotted Tail has consented to be the Beggars' Chief. Those Indians who go over to the white man can be nothing but beggars, for he respects only riches, and how can an Indian be a rich man? He cannot without ceasing to be an Indian. As for me, I have listened patiently to the promises of the Great Father, but his memory is short. I am now done with him. This is all I have to say."

The wilder bands separated soon after this council, to follow the drift of the buffalo, some in the vicinity of the Black Hills and others in the Big Horn region. Small war parties came down from time to time upon stray travelers, who received no mercy at their hands, or made dashes upon neighboring forts. Red Cloud claimed the right to guard and hold by force, if need be, all this territory which had been conceded to his people by the treaty of 1868. The land became a very nest of outlawry. Aside from organized parties of prospectors, there were bands of white horse thieves and desperadoes who took advantage of the situation to plunder immigrants and Indians alike.

An attempt was made by means of military camps to establish control and force all the Indians upon reservations, and another commission was sent to negotiate their removal to Indian Territory, but met with an absolute refusal. After much guerrilla warfare, an important military campaign against the Sioux was set on foot in 1876, ending in Custer's signal defeat upon the Little Big Horn.

In this notable battle, Red Cloud did not participate in person, nor in the earlier one with Crook upon the Little Rosebud, but he had a son in both fights. He was now a councilor rather than a warrior, but his young men were constantly in the field, while Spotted Tail had definitely surrendered and was in close touch with representatives of the government.

But the inevitable end was near. One morning in the fall of 1876 Red Cloud was surrounded by United States troops under the command of Colonel McKenzie, who disarmed his people and brought them into Fort Robinson, Nebraska. Thence they were removed to the Pine Ridge agency, where he lived for more than thirty years as a "reservation Indian." In order to humiliate him further, government authorities proclaimed the more tractable Spotted Tail head chief of the Sioux. Of course, Red Cloud's own people never recognized any other chief.

In 1880 he appealed to Professor Marsh, of Yale, head of a scientific expedition to the Bad Lands, charging certain frauds at the agency and apparently proving his case; at any rate the matter was considered worthy of official investigation. In 1890–1891, during the "Ghost Dance craze" and the difficulties that followed, he was suspected of collusion with the hostiles, but he did not join them openly, and nothing could be proved against him. He was already an old man, and became almost entirely blind before his death in 1909 in his ninetieth year.

His private life was exemplary. He was faithful to one wife all his days, and was a devoted father to his children. He was ambitious for his only son, known as Jack Red Cloud, and much desired him to be a great warrior. He started him on the warpath at the age of fifteen, not then realizing that the days of Indian warfare were well-nigh at an end.

Among latter-day chiefs, Red Cloud was notable as a quiet man, simple and direct in speech, courageous in action, an ardent lover of his country, and possessed in a marked degree of the manly qualities characteristic of the American Indian in his best days.

Spotted Tail

A MONG the Sioux chiefs of the "transition period" only one was shrewd enough to read coming events in their true light. It is said of Spotted Tail that he was rather a slow-moving boy, preferring in their various games and mimic battles to play the rôle of councilor, to plan and assign to the others their parts in the fray. This he did so cleverly that he soon became a leader among his youthful contemporaries; and withal he was apt at mimicry and impersonation, so that the other boys were accustomed to say of him, "He has his grandfather's wit and the wisdom of his grandmother!"

Spotted Tail was an orphan, reared by his grandparents, and at an early age compelled to shift for himself. Thus he was somewhat at a disadvantage among the other boys; yet even this fact may have helped to develop in him courage and ingenuity. One little incident of his boy life, occurring at about his tenth year, is characteristic of the man. In the midst of a game, two boys became involved in a dispute which promised to be a serious one, as both drew knives. The young Spotted Tail instantly began to cry, "The Shoshones are upon us! To arms! to arms!" and the other boys joined in the war whoop. This distracted the attention of the combatants and ended the affair.

Upon the whole, his boyhood is not so well remembered as is that of most of his leading contemporaries, probably because he had no parents to bring him frequently before the people, as was the custom with the well-born, whose every step in their progress toward manhood was publicly announced at a feast given in their honor. It is known, however, that he began at an early age to carve out a position for himself. It is personal qualities alone that tell among our people, and the youthful Spotted Tail gained at every turn. At the age of seventeen, he had become a sure shot and a clever hunter; but, above all, he had already shown that he possessed a superior mind. He had come into contact with white people at the various trading posts, and according to his own story had made a careful study of the white man's habits and modes of thought, especially of his peculiar trait of economy and intense desire to accumulate property. He was accustomed to watch closely and listen attentively whenever any of this strange race had dealings with his people. When a council was held, and the other young men stood at a distance with their robes over their faces so as to avoid recognition, Spotted Tail always put himself in a position to hear all that was said on either side, and weighed all the arguments in his mind.

When he first went upon the warpath, it appears that he was, if anything, over-zealous to establish himself in the eye of his people; and as a matter of fact, it was especially hard for him to gain an assured position among the Brulés, with whom he lived, both because he was an orphan, and because his father had been of another band. Yet it was not long before he had achieved his ambition, though in doing so he received several ugly wounds. It was in a battle with the Utes that he first notably served his people and their cause.

The Utes were the attacking party and far outnumbered the Sioux on this occasion. Many of their bravest young men had fallen, and the Brulés were face to face with utter annihilation, when Spotted Tail, with a handful of daring horsemen, dodged around the enemy's flank and fell upon them from the rear with so much spirit that they supposed that strong reinforcements had arrived, and retreated in confusion. The Sioux pursued on horseback; and it was in this pursuit that the noted chief Two Strike gained his historical name. But the chief honors of the fight belonged to Spotted Tail. The old chiefs, Conquering Bear and the rest, thanked him and at once made him a war chief.

It had been the firm belief of Spotted Tail that it was unwise to allow the white man so much freedom in our country, long before the older chiefs saw any harm in it. After the opening of the Oregon Trail he, above all the others, was watchful of the conduct of the Americans as they journeyed toward the setting sun, and more than once he remarked in council that these white men were not like the French and the Spanish, with whom our old chiefs had been used to deal. He was not fully satisfied with the agreement with General Harney; but as a young warrior who had only just gained his position in the council, he could not force his views upon the older men.

No sooner had the Oregon Trail been secured from the Sioux than Fort Laramie and other frontier posts were strengthened, and the soldiers became more insolent and overbearing than ever. It was soon discovered that the whites were prepared to violate most of the articles of their treaty as the Indians understood it. At this time, the presence of many Mormon emigrants on their way to the settlements in Utah and Wyoming added to the perils of the situation, as they constantly maneuvered for purposes of their own to bring about a clash between the soldiers and the Indians. Every summer there were storm-clouds blowing between these two—clouds usually taking their rise in some affair of the travelers along the trail.

In 1854 an event occurred which has already been described and which snapped the last link of friendship between the races.

By this time Spotted Tail had proved his courage both abroad and at home. He had fought a duel with one of the lesser chiefs, by whom he was attacked. He killed his opponent with an arrow, but himself received upon his head a blow from a battle-axe which brought him senseless to the ground. He was left for dead, but fortunately revived just as the men were preparing his body for burial.

The Brulés sustained him in this quarrel, as he had acted in self-defense; and for a few years he led them in bloody raids against the whites along the historic trail. He ambushed many stagecoaches and emigrant trains, and was responsible for waylaying the Kincaid coach with twenty thousand dollars. This relentless harrying of travelers soon brought General Harney to the Brulé Sioux to demand explanations and reparation.

The old chiefs of the Brulés now appealed to Spotted Tail and his young warriors not to bring any general calamity upon the tribe. To the surprise of all, Spotted Tail declared that he would give himself up. He said that he had defended the rights of his people to the best of his ability, that he had avenged the blood of their chief, Conquering Bear, and that he was not afraid to accept the consequences. He therefore voluntarily surrendered to General Harney, and two of his lieutenants, Red Leaf and Old Woman, followed his example.

Thus Spotted Tail played an important part at the very outset of those events which were soon to overthrow the free life of his people. I do not know how far he foresaw what was to follow; but whether so conceived or not, his surrender was a master stroke, winning for him not only the admiration of his own people but the confidence and respect of the military.

Thus suddenly he found himself in prison, a hostage for the good behavior of his followers. There were many rumors as to the punishment reserved for him; but luckily for Spotted Tail, the promises of General Harney to the Brulé chiefs in respect to him were faithfully kept. One of his fellow-prisoners committed suicide, but the other held out bravely for the two-year term of his imprisonment. During the second year, it was well understood that neither of the men sought to escape, and they were given much freedom. It was fine schooling for Spotted Tail, that tireless observer of the ways of the white man! It is a fact that his engaging personal qualities won for him kindness and sympathy at the fort before the time came for his release.

One day some Indian horse thieves of another tribe stampeded the horses and mules belonging to the garrison. Spotted Tail asked permission of the commanding officer to accompany the pursuers. That officer, trusting in the honor of a Sioux brave, gave him a fast horse and a good carbine, and said to him: "I depend upon you to guide my soldiers so that they may overtake the thieves and recapture the horses!"

The soldiers recaptured the horses without any loss, but Spotted Tail still followed the Indians. When they returned to the fort without him, everybody agreed that he would never turn up. However, next day he did "turn up", with the scalp of one of the marauders!

Soon after this he was returned to his own people, who

honored him by making him the successor of the old chief, Conquering Bear, whose blood he had avenged, for which act he had taken upon himself the full responsibility. He had made good use of his two years at the fort, and completed his studies of civilization to his own satisfaction. From this time on he was desirous of reconciling the Indian and the white man, thoroughly understanding the uselessness of opposition. He was accordingly in constant communication with the military; but the other chiefs did not understand his views and seem to have been suspicious of his motives.

In 1860–1864 the Southern Cheyennes and Comanches were at war with the whites, and some of the Brulés and Ogallalas, who were their neighbors and intimates, were suspected of complicity with the hostiles. Doubtless a few of their young men may have been involved; at any rate, Thunder Bear and Two Face, together with a few others who were roving with the warring tribes, purchased two captive white women and brought them to Fort Laramie. It was, however, reported at the post that these two men had maltreated the women while under their care.

Of course, the commander demanded of Spotted Tail, then head chief, that he give up the guilty ones, and accordingly he had the two men arrested and delivered at the fort. At this there was an outcry among his own people; but he argued that if the charges were true, the men deserved punishment, and if false, they should be tried and cleared by process of law. The Indians never quite knew what evidence was produced at the court-martial, but at all events the two men were hanged, and as they had many influential connections, their relatives lost no time in fomenting trouble. The Sioux were then camping close by the fort and it was midwinter, which facts held them in check for a month or two; but as soon as spring came, they removed their camp across the river and rose in rebellion. A pitched battle was fought, in which the soldiers got the worst of it. Even the associate chief, Big Mouth, was against Spotted Tail, who was practically forced against his will and judgment to take up arms once more.

At this juncture came the sudden and bloody uprising in the east among the Minnesota Sioux, and Sitting Bull's campaign in the north had begun in earnest; while to the south the Southern

Cheyennes, Comanches, and Kiowas were all upon the warpath. Spotted Tail at about this time seems to have conceived the idea of uniting all the Rocky Mountain Indians in a great confederacy. He once said: "Our cause is as a child's cause, in comparison with the power of the white man, unless we can stop quarreling among ourselves and unite our energies for the common good." But old-time antagonisms were too strong; and he was probably held back also by his consciousness of the fact that the Indians called him "the white man's friend", while the military still had some faith in him which he did not care to lose. He was undoubtedly one of the brainiest and most brilliant Sioux who ever lived; and while he could not help being to a large extent in sympathy with the feeling of his race against the invader, yet he alone foresaw the inevitable outcome, and the problem as it presented itself to him was simply this: "What is the best policy to pursue in the existing situation?"

Here is his speech as it has been given to me, delivered at the great council on the Powder River, just before the attack on Fort Phil Kearny. We can imagine that he threw all his wonderful tact and personal magnetism into this last effort at conciliation.

" 'Hay, hay, hay! Alas, alas!' Thus speaks the old man, when he knows that his former vigor and freedom is gone from him forever. So we may exclaim to-day, Alas! There is a time appointed to all things. Think for a moment how many multitudes of the animal tribes we ourselves have destroyed! Look upon the snow that appears to-day—to-morrow it is water! Listen to the dirge of the dry leaves, that were green and vigorous but a few moons before! We are a part of this life and it seems that our time is come.

"Yet note how the decay of one nation invigorates another. This strange white man—consider him, his gifts are manifold! His tireless brain, his busy hand do wonders for his race. Those things which we despise he holds as treasures; yet he is so great and so flourishing that there must be some virtue and truth in his philosophy. I wish to say to you, my friends: Be not moved alone by heated arguments and thoughts of revenge! These are for the young. We are young no longer; let us think well, and give counsel as old men!"

These words were greeted with an ominous silence. Not even the customary "How!" of assent followed the speech, and Sitting Bull immediately got up and replied in the celebrated harangue which will be introduced under his own name in another chapter. The situation was critical for Spotted Tail—the only man present to advocate submission to the stronger race whose ultimate supremacy he recognized as certain. The decision to attack Fort Phil Kearny was unanimous without him, and in order to hold his position among his tribesmen he joined in the charge. Several bullets passed through his war bonnet, and he was slightly wounded.

When the commission of 1867–1868 was sent out to negotiate with the Sioux, Spotted Tail was ready to meet them, and eager to obtain for his people the very best terms that he could. He often puzzled and embarrassed them by his remarkable speeches, the pointed questions that he put, and his telling allusions to former negotiations. Meanwhile Red Cloud would not come into the council until after several deputations of Indians had been sent to him, and Sitting Bull did not come at all.

The famous treaty was signed, and from this time on Spotted Tail never again took up arms against the whites. On the contrary, it was mainly attributed to his influence that the hostiles were subdued much sooner than might have been expected. He came into the reservation with his band, urged his young men to enlist as government scouts, and assisted materially in all negotiations. The hostile chiefs no longer influenced his action, and as soon as they had all been brought under military control, General Crook named Spotted Tail head chief of the Sioux, thus humiliating Red Cloud and arousing jealousy and ill-feeling among the Ogallalas. In order to avoid trouble, he prudently separated himself from the other bands, and moved to the new agency on Beaver Creek (Fort Sheridan, Nebraska), which was called "Spotted Tail Agency."

Just before the daring war leader, Crazy Horse, surrendered to the military, he went down to the agency and roundly rebuked Spotted Tail for signing away the freedom of his people. From the point of view of the irreconcilables, the diplomatic chief was a "trimmer" and a traitor; and many of the Sioux have tried to implicate him in the conspiracy against Crazy Horse which led to his assassination, but I hold that the facts do not bear out this charge. The name of Spotted Tail was prominently before the people during the rest of his life. An obscure orphan, he had achieved distinction by his bravery and sagacity; but he copied the white politician too closely after he entered the reservation. He became a good manipulator, and was made conceited and overbearing by the attentions of the military and of the general public. Furthermore, there was an old feud in his immediate band which affected him closely. Against him for many years were the followers of Big Mouth, whom he had killed in a duel; and also a party led by a son and a nephew of the old chief, Conquering Bear, whom Spotted Tail had succeeded at his death. These two men had hoped that one or the other of them might obtain the succession.

Crow Dog, the nephew of Conquering Bear, more than once taunted Spotted Tail with the fact that he was chief not by the will of the tribe, but by the help of the white soldiers, and told him that he would "keep a bullet for him" in case he ever disgraced his high position. Thus retribution lay in wait for him while at the height of his fame. Several high-handed actions of his at this time, including his elopement with another man's wife, increased his unpopularity with a large element of his own tribe. On the eve of the chief's departure for Washington, to negotiate (or so they suspected) for the sale of more of their land, Crow Dog took up his gun and fulfilled his threat, regarding himself, and regarded by his supporters, not as a murderer, but as an executioner.

Such was the end of the man who may justly be called the Pontiac of the west. He possessed a remarkable mind and extraordinary foresight for an untutored savage; and yet he is the only one of our great men to be remembered with more honor by the white man, perhaps, than by his own people.

Little Crow

CHIEF Little Crow was the eldest son of Cetanwakuwa (Charging Hawk). It was on account of his father's name, mistranslated Crow, that he was called by the whites "Little Crow." His real name was Taoyateduta, His Red People.

As far back as Minnesota history goes, a band of the Sioux called Kaposia (Light Weight, because they were said to travel light) inhabited the Mille Lacs region. Later they dwelt about St. Croix Falls, and still later near St. Paul. In 1840, Cetanwakuwa was still living in what is now West St. Paul, but he was soon after killed by the accidental discharge of his gun.

It was during a period of demoralization for the Kaposias that Little Crow became the leader of his people. His father, a well-known chief, had three wives, all from different bands of the Sioux. He was the only son of the first wife, a Leaf Dweller. There were two sons of the second and two of the third wife, and the second set of brothers conspired to kill their half-brother in order to keep the chieftainship in the family.

Two kegs of whisky were bought, and all the men of the tribe invited to a feast. It was planned to pick some sort of quarrel when all were drunk, and in the confusion Little Crow was to be murdered. The plot went smoothly until the last instant, when a young brave saved the intended victim by knocking the gun aside with his hatchet, so that the shot went wild. However, it broke his right arm, which remained crooked all his life. The friends of the young chieftain hastily withdrew, avoiding a general fight; and later the council of the Kaposias condemned the two

19

brothers, both of whom were executed, leaving him in undisputed possession.

Such was the opening of a stormy career. Little Crow's mother had been a chief's daughter, celebrated for her beauty and spirit, and it is said that she used to plunge him into the lake through a hole in the ice, rubbing him afterward with snow, to strengthen his nerves, and that she would remain with him alone in the deep woods for days at a time, so that he might know that solitude is good, and not fear to be alone with nature.

"My son," she would say, "if you are to be a leader of men, you must listen in silence to the mystery, the spirit."

At a very early age she made a feast for her boy and announced that he would fast two days. This is what might be called a formal presentation to the spirit or God. She greatly desired him to become a worthy leader according to the ideas of her people. It appears that she left her husband when he took a second wife, and lived with her own band till her death. She did not marry again.

Little Crow was an intensely ambitious man and without physical fear. He was always in perfect training and early acquired the art of warfare of the Indian type. It is told of him that when he was about ten years old, he engaged with other boys in a sham battle on the shore of a lake near St. Paul. Both sides were encamped at a little distance from one another, and the rule was that the enemy must be surprised, otherwise the attack would be considered a failure. One must come within so many paces undiscovered in order to be counted successful. Our hero had a favorite dog which, at his earnest request, was allowed to take part in the game, and as a scout he entered the enemy camp unseen, by the help of his dog.

When he was twelve, he saved the life of a companion who had broken through the ice by tying the end of a pack line to a log, then, at great risk to himself, carrying it to the edge of the hole where his comrade went down. It is said that he also broke in, but both boys saved themselves by means of the line.

As a young man, Little Crow was always ready to serve his people as a messenger to other tribes, a duty involving much danger and hardship. He was also known as one of the best hunters in his band. Although still young, he had already a war record when he became chief of the Kaposias, at a time when the Sioux were facing the greatest and most far-reaching changes that had ever come to them.

At this juncture in the history of the northwest and its native inhabitants, the various fur companies had paramount influence. They did not hesitate to impress the Indians with the idea that they were the authorized representatives of the white races or peoples, and they were quick to realize the desirability of controlling the natives through their most influential chiefs. Little Crow became quite popular with post traders and factors. He was an orator as well as a diplomat, and one of the first of his nation to indulge in politics and promote unstable schemes to the detriment of his people.

When the United States Government went into the business of acquiring territory from the Indians so that the flood of western settlement might not be checked, commissions were sent out to negotiate treaties, and in case of failure it often happened that a delegation of leading men of the tribe were invited to Washington. At that period, these visiting chiefs, attired in all the splendor of their costumes of ceremony, were treated like ambassadors from foreign countries.

One winter in the late eighteen-fifties, a major general of the army gave a dinner to the Indian chiefs then in the city, and on this occasion Little Crow was appointed toastmaster. There were present a number of Senators and members of Congress, as well as judges of the Supreme Court, cabinet officers, and other distinguished citizens. When all the guests were seated, the Sioux arose and addressed them with much dignity as follows:

"Warriors and friends: I am informed that the great white war chief who of his generosity and comradeship has given us this feast, has expressed the wish that we may follow to-night the usages and customs of my people. In other words, this is a warriors' feast, a braves' meal. I call upon the Ojibway chief, the Hole-in-the-Day, to give the lone wolf's hunger call, after which we will join him in our usual manner."

The tall and handsome Ojibway now rose and straightened his superb form to utter one of the clearest and longest wolf howls that was ever heard in Washington, and at its close came a tremendous burst of war whoops that fairly rent the air, and no doubt electrified the officials there present.

On one occasion Little Crow was invited by the commander of Fort Ridgeley, Minnesota, to call at the fort. On his way back, in company with a half-breed named Ross and the interpreter Mitchell, he was ambushed by a party of Ojibways, and again wounded in the same arm that had been broken in his attempted assassination. His companion Ross was killed, but he managed to hold the war party at bay until help came and thus saved his life.

More and more as time passed, this naturally brave and ambitious man became a prey to the selfish interests of the traders and politicians. The immediate causes of the Sioux outbreak of 1862 came in quick succession to inflame to desperate action an outraged people. The two bands on the so-called "lower reservations" in Minnesota were Indians for whom nature had provided most abundantly in their free existence. After one hundred and fifty years of friendly intercourse first with the French, then the English, and finally the Americans, they found themselves cut off from every natural resource, on a tract of land twenty miles by thirty, which to them was virtual imprisonment. By treaty stipulation with the government, they were to be fed and clothed, houses were to be built for them, the men taught agriculture, and schools provided for the children. In addition to this, a trust fund of a million and a half was to be set aside for them, at five per cent interest, the interest to be paid annually per capita. They had signed the treaty under pressure, believing in these promises on the faith of a great nation.

However, on entering the new life, the resources so rosily described to them failed to materialize. Many families faced starvation every winter, their only support the store of the Indian trader, who was baiting his trap for their destruction. Very gradually they awoke to the facts. At last it was planned to secure from them the north half of their reservation for ninety-eight thousand dollars, but it was not explained to the Indians that the traders were to receive all the money. Little Crow made the greatest mistake of his life when he signed this agreement.

Meanwhile, to make matters worse, the cash annuities were

not paid for nearly two years. Civil War had begun. When it was learned that the traders had taken all of the ninety-eight thousand dollars "on account", there was very bitter feeling. In fact, the heads of the leading stores were afraid to go about as usual, and most of them stayed in St. Paul. Little Crow was justly held in part responsible for the deceit, and his life was not safe.

The murder of a white family near Acton, Minnesota, by a party of Indian duck hunters in August, 1862, precipitated the break. Messengers were sent to every village with the news, and at the villages of Little Crow and Little Six the war council was red-hot. It was proposed to take advantage of the fact that north and south were at war to wipe out the white settlers and to regain their freedom. A few men stood out against such a desperate step, but the conflagration had gone beyond their control.

There were many mixed bloods among these Sioux, and some of the Indians held that these were accomplices of the white people in robbing them of their possessions, therefore their lives should not be spared. My father, Many Lightnings, who was practically the leader of the Mankato band (for Mankato, the chief, was a weak man), fought desperately for the lives of the half-breeds and the missionaries. The chiefs had great confidence in my father, yet they would not commit themselves, since their braves were clamoring for blood. Little Crow had been accused of all the misfortunes of his tribe, and he now hoped by leading them against the whites to regain his prestige with his people, and a part at least of their lost domain.

There were moments when the pacifists were in grave peril. It was almost day-break when my father saw that the approaching calamity could not be prevented. He and two others said to Little Crow: "If you want war, you must personally lead your men to-morrow. We will not murder women and children, but we will fight the soldiers when they come." They then left the council and hastened to warn my brother-in-law, Faribault, and others who were in danger.

Little Crow declared he would be seen in the front of every battle, and it is true that he was foremost in all the succeeding bloodshed, urging his warriors to spare none. He ordered his war leader, Many Hail, to fire the first shot, killing the trader James Lynd, in the door of his store.

After a year of fighting in which he had met with defeat, the discredited chief retreated to Fort Garry, now Winnipeg, Manitoba, where, together with Standing Buffalo, he undertook secret negotiations with his old friends the Indian traders. There was now a price upon his head, but he planned to reach St. Paul undetected and there surrender himself to his friends, who he hoped would protect him in return for past favors. It is true that he had helped them to secure perhaps the finest country held by any Indian nation for a mere song.

He left Canada with a few trusted friends, including his youngest and favorite son. When within two or three days' journey of St. Paul, he told the others to return, keeping with him only his son, Wowinape, who was but fifteen years of age. He meant to steal into the city by night and go straight to Governor Ramsey, who was his personal friend. He was very hungry and was obliged to keep to the shelter of the deep woods. The next morning, as he was picking and eating wild raspberries, he was seen by a woodchopper named Lamson. The man did not know who he was. He only knew that he was an Indian, and that was enough for him, so he lifted his rifle to his shoulder and fired, then ran at his best pace. The brilliant but misguided chief, who had made that part of the country unsafe for any white man to live in, sank to the ground and died without a struggle. The boy took his father's gun and made some effort to find the assassin, but as he did not even know in which direction to look for him, he soon gave up the attempt and went back to his friends.

Meanwhile Lamson reached home breathless and made his report. The body of the chief was found and identified, in part by the twice broken arm, and this arm and his scalp may be seen to-day in the collection of the Minnesota Historical Society.

Tamahay

THERE was once a Sioux brave who declared that he would
die young, yet not by his own hand. Tamahay was of heroic
proportions, herculean in strength, a superb runner; in fact, he
had all the physical qualities of an athlete or a typical Indian. In
his scanty dress, he was beautiful as an antique statue in living
bronze. When a mere youth, seventeen years of age, he met with
an accident which determined his career. It was the loss of an
eye, a fatal injury to the sensitive and high-spirited Indian. He
announced his purpose in these words:

"The 'Great Mystery' has decreed that I must be disgraced.
There will be no pleasure for me now, and I shall be ridiculed
even by my enemies. It will be well for me to enter soon into
Paradise, for I shall be happy in spending my youth there. But
I will sell my life dearly. Hereafter my name shall be spoken in
the traditions of our race." With this speech Tamahay began his
career.

He now sought glory and defied danger with even more than
the ordinary Indian recklessness. He accepted a personal friend,
which was a custom among the Sioux, where each man chose a
companion for life and death. The tie was stronger than one of
blood relationship, a friendship sealed by solemn vow and cov-
enant. Tamahay's intimate was fortunately almost his equal in
physical powers, and the pair became the terror of neighboring
tribes, with whom the Dakotas were continually at war. They
made frequent raids upon their enemies and were usually successful, although not without thrilling experiences and almost
miraculous escapes.

Upon one of these occasions the two friends went north into the country of the Ojibways. After many days' journey, they discovered a small village of the foe. The wicked Tamahay proposed to his associate that they should arrange their toilets after the fashion of the Ojibways, and go among them; "and perhaps," he added, "we will indulge in a little flirtation with their pretty maids, and when we have had enough of the fun we can take the scalp of a brave or two and retreat!" His friend construed his daring proposition to be a test of courage, which it would not become him, as a brave, to decline; therefore he assented with a show of cheerfulness.

The handsome strangers were well received by the Ojibway girls, but their perilous amusement was brought to an untimely close. A young maiden prematurely discovered their true characters, and her cry of alarm brought instantly to her side a jealous youth, who had been watching them from his place of concealment. With him Tamahay had a single-handed contest, and before a general alarm was given he had dispatched the foe and fled with his scalp.

The unfortunate brave had been a favorite and a leader among the tribe; therefore the maddened Ojibways were soon in hot pursuit. The Sioux braves were fine runners, yet they were finally driven out upon the peninsula of a lake. As they became separated in their retreat, Tamahay shouted, "I'll meet you at the mouth of the St. Croix River, or in the spirit land!" Both managed to swim the lake, and so made good their escape.

The exploits of this man were not all of a warlike nature. He was a great traveler and an expert scout, and he had some wonderful experiences with wild animals. He was once sent, with his intimate friend, on a scout for game. They were on ponies.

They located a herd of buffaloes, and on their return to the camp espied a lonely buffalo. Tamahay suggested that they should chase it in order to take some fresh meat, as the law of the tribe allowed in the case of a single animal. His pony stumbled and threw him, after they had wounded the bison, and the latter attacked the dismounted man viciously. But he, as usual, was on the alert. He "took the bull by the horns", as the saying is, and cleverly straddled him on the neck. The buffalo had no means of harming his enemy, but pawed the earth and struggled until his strength was exhausted, when the Indian used his knife on the animal's throat. On account of this feat he received the name "Held-the-Bull-by-the-Horns."

The origin of his name "Tamahay" is related as follows. When he was a young man he accompanied the chief Wabashaw to Mackinaw, Michigan, together with some other warriors. He was out with his friend one day, viewing the wonderful sights in the "white man's country", when they came upon a sow with her numerous pink little progeny. He was greatly amused and picked up one of the young pigs, but as soon as it squealed the mother ran furiously after them. He kept the pig and fled with it, still laughing; but his friend was soon compelled to run up the conveniently inclined trunk of a fallen tree, while our hero reached the shore of a lake near by, and plunged into the water. He swam and dived as long as he could, but the beast continued to threaten him with her sharp teeth, till, almost exhausted, he swam again to shore, where his friend came up and dispatched the vicious animal with a club. On account of this watery adventure he was at once called Tamahay, meaning Pike. He earned many other names, but preferred this one, because it was the name borne by a great friend of his, Lieutenant Pike, the first officer of the United States Army who came to Minnesota for the purpose of exploring the sources of the Mississippi River and of making peace with the natives. Tamahay assisted this officer in obtaining land from the Sioux upon which to build Fort Snelling. He appears in history under the name of "Tahamie" or the "One-Eyed Sioux."

Always ready to brave danger and unpopularity, Tamahay was the only Sioux who sided with the United States in her struggle with Great Britain in 1812. For having espoused the cause of the Americans, he was ill-treated by the British officers and free traders, who for a long time controlled the northwest, even after peace had been effected between the two nations. At one time he was confined in a fort called McKay, where now stands the town of Prairie du Chien, Wisconsin. He had just returned from St. Louis, and was suspected of exciting his people to rebel against British subjects. His life was even threatened, but to this

Tamahay merely replied that he was ready to die. A few months later, this fort was restored to the United States, and upon leaving it the British set the buildings on fire, though the United States flag floated above them. Some Indians who were present shouted to Tamahay, "Your friends', the Americans', fort is on fire!" He responded with a war whoop, rushed into the blazing fort, and brought out the flag. For this brave act he was rewarded with a present of a flag and medal. He was never tired of displaying this medal and his recommendation papers, and even preserved to the end of his life an old colonial stovepipe hat, which he wore upon state occasions.

The Sioux long referred to the president of the United States as "Tamahay's father."

The following story is told of him in his later days. He attempted one day to cross the first bridge over the Mississippi River, but was not recognized by the sentinel, who would not allow him to pass until he paid the toll. Tamahay, who was a privileged character, explained as best he could, with gestures and broken English, that he was always permitted to pass free; but as the sentinel still refused, and even threatened him with his bayonet, the old Indian silently seized the musket, threw it down into the waters of the Mississippi and went home. Later in the day a company of soldiers appeared in the Indian village, and escorted our hero to a sort of court-martial at the fort. When he was questioned by the Colonel, he simply replied: "If you were threatened by any one with a weapon, you would, in self-defense, either disable the man or get rid of the weapon. I did the latter, thinking that you would need the man more than the gun."

Finally the officer said to them, "I see you are both partly wrong. Some one must be responsible for the loss of the gun; therefore, you two will wrestle, and the man who is downed must dive for the weapon to the bottom of the river."

Scarcely was this speech ended when Tamahay was upon the soldier, who was surprised both by the order and by the unexpected readiness of the wily old Indian, so that he was not prepared, and the Sioux had the vantage hold. In a moment the bluecoat was down, amid shouts and peals of laughter from his comrades. Having thrown his man, the other turned and went home without a word.

Sad to say, he acquired a great appetite for "minne-wakan", or "mysterious water", as the Sioux call it, which proved a source of trouble to him in his old age. It is told of him that he was treated one winter's day to a drink of whisky in a trader's store. He afterwards went home; but even the severe blizzard which soon arose did not prevent him from returning in the night to the friendly trader. He awoke that worthy from sleep about twelve o'clock by singing his death dirge upon the roof of the log cabin. In another moment he had jumped down the mud chimney, and into the blazing embers of a fire. The trader had to pour out to him some whisky in a tin pail, after which he begged the old man to "be good and go home." On the eve of the so-called "Minnesota Massacre" by the Sioux in 1862, Tamahay, although he was then very old and had almost lost the use of his remaining eye, made a famous speech at the meeting of the conspirators. These are some of his words, as reported to me by persons who were present.

"What! What! is this Little Crow? Is that Little Six? You, too, White Dog, are you here? I cannot see well now, but I can see with my mind's eye the stream of blood you are about to pour upon the bosom of this mother of ours" (meaning the earth). "I stand before you on three legs, but the third leg has brought me wisdom" [referring to the staff with which he supported himself]. "I have traveled much, I have visited among the people whom you think to defy. This means the total surrender of our beautiful land, the land of a thousand lakes and streams. Methinks you are about to commit an act like that of the porcupine, who climbs a tree, balances himself upon a springy bough, and then gnaws off the very bough upon which he is sitting; hence, when it gives way, he falls upon the sharp rocks below. Behold the great Pontiac, whose grave I saw near St. Louis; he was murdered while an exile from his country! Think of the brave Black Hawk! Methinks his spirit is still wailing through Wisconsin and Illinois for his lost people! I do not say you have no cause to complain, but to resist is self-destruction. I am done."

It is supposed that this speech was his last, and it was made, though vainly, in defense of the Americans whom he had loved. He died at Fort Pierre, South Dakota, in 1864. His people say that he died a natural death, of old age. And yet his exploits are not forgotten. Thus lived and departed a most active and fearless Sioux, Tamahay, who desired to die young!

Gall

CHIEF Gall was one of the most aggressive leaders of the Sioux nation in their last stand for freedom.

The westward pressure of civilization during the past three centuries has been tremendous. When our hemisphere was "discovered", it had been inhabited by the natives for untold ages, but it was held undiscovered because the original owners did not chart or advertise it. Yet some of them at least had developed ideals of life which included *real* liberty and equality to all men, and they did not recognize individual ownership in land or other property beyond actual necessity. It was a soul development leading to essential manhood. Under this system they brought forth some striking characters.

Gall was considered by both Indians and whites to be a most impressive type of physical manhood. From his picture you can judge of this for yourself.

Let us follow his trail. He was no tenderfoot. He never asked a soft place for himself. He always played the game according to the rules and to a finish. To be sure, like every other man, he made some mistakes, but he was an Indian and never acted the coward.

The earliest stories told of his life and doings indicate the spirit of the man in that of the boy.

When he was only about three years old, the Blackfoot band of Sioux were on their usual roving hunt, following the buffalo while living their natural happy life upon the wonderful wide prairies of the Dakotas.

It was the way of every Sioux mother to adjust her household effects on such dogs and pack ponies as she could muster from day to day, often lending one or two to accommodate some other woman whose horse or dog had died, or perhaps had been among those stampeded and carried away by a raiding band of Crow warriors. On this particular occasion, the mother of our young Sioux brave, Matohinshda, or Bear-Shedding-His-Hair (Gall's childhood name), intrusted her boy to an old Eskimo pack dog, experienced and reliable, except perhaps when unduly excited or very thirsty.

On the day of removing camp the caravan made its morning march up the Powder River. Upon the wide table-land the women were busily digging teepsinna (an edible sweetish root, much used by them) as the moving village slowly progressed. As usual at such times, the trail was wide. An old jack rabbit had waited too long in hiding. Now, finding himself almost surrounded by the mighty plains people, he sprang up suddenly, his feathery ears conspicuously erect, a dangerous challenge to the dogs and the people.

A whoop went up. Every dog accepted the challenge. Forgotten were the bundles, the kits, even the babies they were drawing or carrying. The chase was on, and the screams of the women reëchoed from the opposite cliffs of the Powder, mingled with the yelps of dogs and the neighing of horses. The hand of every man was against the daring warrior, the lone Jack, and the confusion was great.

When the fleeing one cleared the mass of his enemies, he emerged with a swiftness that commanded respect and gave promise of a determined chase. Behind him, his pursuers stretched out in a thin line, first the speedy, unburdened dogs and then the travois dogs headed by the old Eskimo with his precious freight. The youthful Gall was in a travois, a basket mounted on trailing poles and harnessed to the sides of the animal.

"Hey! hey! they are gaining on him!" a warrior shouted. At this juncture two of the canines had almost nabbed their furry prey by the back. But he was too cunning for them. He dropped instantly and sent both dogs over his head, rolling and spinning, then made another flight at right angles to the first. This gave the Eskimo a chance to cut the triangle. He gained fifty yards, but being heavily handicapped, two unladen dogs passed him. The same trick was repeated by the Jack, and this time he saved himself from instant death by a double loop and was now running directly toward the crowd, followed by a dozen or more dogs. He was losing speed, but likewise his pursuers were dropping off steadily. Only the sturdy Eskimo dog held to his even gait, and behind him in the frail travois leaned forward the little Matohinshda, nude save a breech clout, his left hand holding fast the convenient tail of his dog, the right grasping firmly one of the poles of the travois. His black eyes were bulging almost out of their sockets; his long hair flowed out behind like a stream of dark water.

The Jack now ran directly toward the howling spectators, but his marvelous speed and alertness were on the wane; while on the other hand his foremost pursuer, who had taken part in hundreds of similar events, had every confidence in his own endurance. Each leap brought him nearer, fiercer and more determined. The last effort of the Jack was to lose himself in the crowd, like a fish in muddy water; but the big dog made the one needed leap with unerring aim and his teeth flashed as he caught the rabbit in viselike jaws and held him limp in air, a victor!

The people rushed up to him as he laid the victim down, and foremost among them was the frantic mother of Matohinshda, or Gall. "Michinkshe! michinkshe!" (My son! my son!) she screamed as she drew near. The boy seemed to be none the worse for his experience. "Mother!" he cried, "my dog is brave: he got the rabbit!" She snatched him off the travois, but he struggled out of her arms to look upon his dog lovingly and admiringly. Old men and boys crowded about the hero of the day, the dog, and the thoughtful grandmother of Matohinshda unharnessed him and poured some water from a parfleche water bag into a basin. "Here, my grandson, give your friend something to drink."

"How, hechetu," pronounced an old warrior no longer in active service. "This may be only an accident, an ordinary affair; but such things sometimes indicate a career. The boy has had a wonderful ride. I prophesy that he will one day hold the attention of all the people with his doings."

This is the first remembered story of the famous chief, but other boyish exploits foretold the man he was destined to be. He fought many sham battles, some successful and others not; but he was always a fierce fighter and a good loser.

Once he was engaged in a battle with snowballs. There were probably nearly a hundred boys on each side, and the rule was that every fair hit made the receiver officially dead. He must not participate further, but must remain just where he was struck.

Gall's side was fast losing, and the battle was growing hotter every minute when the youthful warrior worked toward an old water hole and took up his position there. His side was soon annihilated and there were eleven men left to fight him. He was pressed close in the wash-out, and as he dodged under cover before a volley of snowballs, there suddenly emerged in his stead a huge gray wolf. His opponents fled in every direction in superstitious terror, for they thought he had been transformed into the animal. To their astonishment he came out on the farther side and ran to the line of safety, a winner!

It happened that the wolf's den had been partly covered with snow so that no one had noticed it until the yells of the boys aroused the inmate, and he beat a hasty retreat. The boys always looked upon this incident as an omen.

Gall had an amiable disposition but was quick to resent insult or injustice. This sometimes involved him in difficulties, but he seldom fought without good cause and was popular with his associates. One of his characteristics was his ability to organize, and this was a large factor in his leadership when he became a man. He was tried in many ways, and never was known to hesitate when it was a question of physical courage and endurance. He entered the public service early in life, but not until he had proved himself competent and passed all tests.

When a mere boy, he was once scouting for game in midwinter, far from camp, and was overtaken by a three days' blizzard. He was forced to abandon his horse and lie under the snow for that length of time. He afterward said he was not particularly hungry; it was thirst and stiffness from which he suffered most. One reason the Indian so loved his horse or dog was that at such times the animal would stay by him like a brother. On this occasion Gall's pony was not more than a stone's throw away when the storm subsided and the sun shone. There was a herd of buffalo in plain sight, and the young hunter was not long in procuring a meal.

This chief's contemporaries still recall his wrestling match with the equally powerful Cheyenne boy, Roman Nose, who afterward became a chief well known to American history. It was a custom of the northwestern Indians, when two friendly tribes camped together, to establish the physical and athletic supremacy of the youth of the respective camps.

The "Che-hoo-hoo" is a wrestling game in which there may be any number on a side, but the numbers are equal. All the boys of each camp are called together by a leader chosen for the purpose and draw themselves up in line of battle; then each at a given signal attacks his opponent.

In this memorable contest, Matohinshda, or Gall, was placed opposite Roman Nose. The whole people turned out as spectators of the struggle, and the battlefield was a plateau between the two camps, in the midst of picturesque Bad Lands. There were many athletic youths present, but these two were really the Apollos of the two tribes.

In this kind of sport it is not allowed to strike with the hand, nor catch around the neck, nor kick, nor pull by the hair. One may break away and run a few yards to get a fresh start, or clinch, or catch as catch can. When a boy is thrown and held to the ground, he is counted out. If a boy has met his superior, he may drop to the ground to escape rough handling, but it is very seldom one gives up without a full trial of strength.

It seemed almost like a real battle, so great was the enthusiasm, as the shouts of sympathizers on both sides went up in a mighty chorus. At last all were either conquerors or subdued except Gall and Roman Nose. The pair seemed equally matched. Both were stripped to the breech clout, now tugging like two young buffalo or elk in mating time, again writhing and twisting like serpents. At times they fought like two wild stallions, straining every muscle of arms, legs, and back in the struggle. Every now and then one was lifted off his feet for a moment, but came down planted like a tree, and after swaying to and fro soon became rigid again.

All eyes were upon the champions. Finally, either by trick or main force, Gall laid the other sprawling upon the ground and held him fast for a minute, then released him and stood erect, panting, a master youth. Shout after shout went up on the Sioux side of the camp. The mother of Roman Nose came forward and threw a superbly worked buffalo robe over Gall, whose mother returned the compliment by covering the young Cheyenne with a handsome blanket.

Undoubtedly these early contests had their influence upon our hero's career. It was his habit to appear most opportunely in a crisis, and in a striking and dramatic manner to take command of the situation. The best known example of this is his entrance on the scene of confusion when Reno surprised the Sioux on the Little Big Horn. Many of the excitable youths, almost unarmed, rushed madly and blindly to meet the intruder, and the scene might have unnerved even an experienced warrior. It was Gall, with not a garment upon his superb body, who on his black charger dashed ahead of the boys and faced them. He stopped them on the dry creek, while the bullets of Reno's men whistled about their ears. "Hold hard, men! Steady, we are not ready yet! Wait for more guns, more horses, and the day is yours!"

They obeyed, and in a few minutes the signal to charge was given, and Reno retreated pell mell before the onset of the Sioux.

Sitting Bull had confidence in his men so long as Gall planned and directed the attack, whether against United States soldiers or the warriors of another tribe. He was a strategist, and able in a twinkling to note and seize upon an advantage. He was really the mainstay of Sitting Bull's effective last stand. He consistently upheld his people's right to their buffalo plains and believed that they should hold the government strictly to its agreements with them. When the treaty of 1868 was disregarded, he agreed with Sitting Bull in defending the last of their once vast domain, and after the Custer battle entered Canada with his chief. They hoped to bring their lost cause before the English government and were much disappointed when they were asked to return to the United States.

Gall finally reported at Fort Peck, Montana, in 1881, and brought half of the Hunkpapa band with him, whereupon he was soon followed by Sitting Bull himself. Although they had been promised by the United States commission who went to

Canada to treat with them that they would not be punished if they returned, no sooner had Gall come down than a part of his people were attacked, and in the spring they were all brought to Fort Randall and held as military prisoners. From this point they were returned to Standing Rock agency.

When "Buffalo Bill" successfully launched his first show, he made every effort to secure both Sitting Bull and Gall for his leading attractions. The military was in complete accord with him in this, for they still had grave suspicions of these two leaders. While Sitting Bull reluctantly agreed, Gall haughtily said: "I am not an animal to be exhibited before the crowd," and retired to his teepee. His spirit was much worn, and he lost strength from that time on. That superb manhood dwindled, and in a few years he died. He was a real hero of a free and natural people, a type that is never to be seen again.

Crazy Horse

CRAZY Horse was born on the Republican River about 1845. He was killed at Fort Robinson, Nebraska, in 1877, so that he lived barely thirty-three years.

He was an uncommonly handsome man. While not the equal of Gall in magnificence and imposing stature, he was physically perfect, an Apollo in symmetry. Furthermore he was a true type of Indian refinement and grace. He was modest and courteous as Chief Joseph; the difference is that he was a born warrior, while Joseph was not. However, he was a gentle warrior, a true brave, who stood for the highest ideal of the Sioux. Notwithstanding all that biased historians have said of him, it is only fair to judge a man by the estimate of his own people rather than that of his enemies.

The boyhood of Crazy Horse was passed in the days when the western Sioux saw a white man but seldom, and then it was usually a trader or a soldier. He was carefully brought up according to the tribal customs. At that period the Sioux prided themselves on the training and development of their sons and daughters, and not a step in that development was overlooked as an excuse to bring the child before the public by giving a feast in its honor. At such times the parents often gave so generously to the needy that they almost impoverished themselves, thus setting an example to the child of self-denial for the general good. His first step alone, the first word spoken, first game killed, the attainment of manhood or womanhood, each was the occasion of a feast and dance in his honor, at which the poor always benefited to the full extent of the parents' ability.

Big-heartedness, generosity, courage, and self-denial are the qualifications of a public servant, and the average Indian was keen to follow this ideal. As every one knows, these characteristic traits become a weakness when he enters a life founded upon commerce and gain. Under such conditions the life of Crazy Horse began. His mother, like other mothers, tender and watchful of her boy, would never once place an obstacle in the way of his father's severe physical training. They laid the spiritual and patriotic foundations of his education in such a way that he early became conscious of the demands of public service.

He was perhaps four or five years old when the band was snowed in one severe winter. They were very short of food, but his father was a tireless hunter. The buffalo, their main dependence, were not to be found, but he was out in the storm and cold every day and finally brought in two antelopes. The little boy got on his pet pony and rode through the camp, telling the old folks to come to his mother's teepee for meat. It turned out that neither his father nor mother had authorized him to do this. Before they knew it, old men and women were lined up before the teepee home, ready to receive the meat, in answer to his invitation. As a result, the mother had to distribute nearly all of it, keeping only enough for two meals.

On the following day the child asked for food. His mother told him that the old folks had taken it all, and added: "Remember, my son, they went home singing praises in your name, not my name or your father's. You must be brave. You must live up to your reputation."

Crazy Horse loved horses, and his father gave him a pony of his own when he was very young. He became a fine horseman and accompanied his father on buffalo hunts, holding the pack horses while the men chased the buffalo and thus gradually learning the art. In those days the Sioux had but few guns, and the hunting was mostly done with bow and arrows.

Another story told of his boyhood is that when he was about twelve he went to look for the ponies with his little brother, whom he loved much, and took a great deal of pains to teach what he had already learned. They came to some wild cherry trees full of ripe fruit, and while they were enjoying it, the brothers were startled by the growl and sudden rush of a bear. Young Crazy Horse pushed his brother up into the nearest tree and himself sprang upon the back of one of the horses, which was frightened and ran some distance before he could control him. As soon as he could, however, he turned him about and came back, yelling and swinging his lariat over his head. The bear at first showed fight but finally turned and ran. The old man who told me this story added that young as he was, he had some power, so that even a grizzly did not care to tackle him. I believe it is a fact that a silver-tip will dare anything except a bell or a lasso line, so that accidentally the boy had hit upon the very thing which would drive him off.

It was usual for Sioux boys of his day to wait in the field after a buffalo hunt until sundown, when the young calves would come out in the open, hungrily seeking their mothers. Then these wild children would enjoy a mimic hunt, and lasso the calves or drive them into camp. Crazy Horse was found to be a determined little fellow, and it was settled one day among the larger boys that they would "stump" him to ride a good-sized bull calf. He rode the calf, and stayed on its back while it ran bawling over the hills, followed by the other boys on their ponies, until his strange mount stood trembling and exhausted.

At the age of sixteen he joined a war party against the Gros Ventres. He was well in the front of the charge, and at once established his bravery by following closely one of the foremost Sioux warriors, by the name of Hump, drawing the enemy's fire and circling around their advance guard. Suddenly Hump's horse was shot from under him, and there was a rush of warriors to kill or capture him while down. But amidst a shower of arrows the youth leaped from his pony, helped his friend into his own saddle, sprang up behind him, and carried him off in safety, although they were hotly pursued by the enemy. Thus he associated himself in his maiden battle with the wizard of Indian warfare, and Hump, who was then at the height of his own career, pronounced Crazy Horse the coming warrior of the Teton Sioux.

At this period of his life, as was customary with the best young men, he spent much time in prayer and solitude. Just what happened in these days of his fasting in the wilderness and upon the crown of bald buttes, no one will ever know; for these things may only be known when one has lived through the battles of life to an honored old age. He was much sought after by his youthful associates, but was noticeably reserved and modest; yet in the moment of danger he at once rose above them all—a natural leader! Crazy Horse was a typical Sioux brave, and from the point of view of our race an ideal hero, living at the height of the epical progress of the American Indian and maintaining in his own character all that was most subtle and ennobling of their spiritual life, and that has since been lost in the contact with a material civilization.

He loved Hump, that peerless warrior, and the two became close friends, in spite of the difference in age. Men called them "the grizzly and his cub." Again and again the pair saved the day for the Sioux in a skirmish with some neighboring tribe. But one day they undertook a losing battle against the Snakes. The Sioux were in full retreat and were fast being overwhelmed by superior numbers. The old warrior fell in a last desperate charge; but Crazy Horse and his younger brother, though dismounted, killed two of the enemy and thus made good their retreat.

It was observed of him that when he pursued the enemy into their stronghold, as he was wont to do, he often refrained from killing, and simply struck them with a switch, showing that he did not fear their weapons nor care to waste his upon them. In attempting this very feat, he lost this only brother of his, who emulated him closely. A party of young warriors, led by Crazy Horse, had dashed upon a frontier post, killed one of the sentinels, stampeded the horses, and pursued the herder to the very gate of the stockade, thus drawing upon themselves the fire of the garrison. The leader escaped without a scratch, but his young brother was brought down from his horse and killed.

While he was still under twenty, there was a great winter buffalo hunt, and he came back with ten buffaloes' tongues which he sent to the council lodge for the councilors' feast. He had in one winter day killed ten buffalo cows with his bow and arrows, and the unsuccessful hunters or those who had no swift ponies were made happy by his generosity. When the hunters returned, these came chanting songs of thanks. He knew that his father was an expert hunter and had a good horse, so he took no meat home, putting in practice the spirit of his early teaching.

He attained his majority at the crisis of the difficulties between the United States and the Sioux. Even before that time, Crazy Horse had already proved his worth to his people in Indian warfare. He had risked his life again and again, and in some instances it was considered almost a miracle that he had saved others as well as himself. He was no orator nor was he the son of a chief. His success and influence was purely a matter of personality. He had never fought the whites up to this time, and indeed no "coup" was counted for killing or scalping a white man.

Young Crazy Horse was twenty-one years old when all the Teton Sioux chiefs (the western or plains dwellers) met in council to determine upon their future policy toward the invader. Their former agreements had been by individual bands, each for itself, and every one was friendly. They reasoned that the country was wide, and that the white traders should be made welcome. Up to this time they had anticipated no conflict. They had permitted the Oregon Trail, but now to their astonishment forts were built and garrisoned in their territory.

Most of the chiefs advocated a strong resistance. There were a few influential men who desired still to live in peace, and who were willing to make another treaty. Among these were White Bull, Two Kettle, Four Bears, and Swift Bear. Even Spotted Tail, afterward the great peace chief, was at this time with the majority, who decided in the year 1866 to defend their rights and territory by force. Attacks were to be made upon the forts within their country and on every trespasser on the same.

Crazy Horse took no part in the discussion, but he and all the young warriors were in accord with the decision of the council. Although so young, he was already a leader among them. Other prominent young braves were Sword (brother of the man of that name who was long captain of police at Pine Ridge), the younger Hump, Charging Bear, Spotted Elk, Crow King, No Water, Big Road, He Dog, the nephew of Red Cloud, and Touch-the-Cloud, intimate friend of Crazy Horse.

The attack on Fort Phil Kearny was the first fruits of the new policy, and here Crazy Horse was chosen to lead the attack on the woodchoppers, designed to draw the soldiers out of the fort, while an army of six hundred lay in wait for them. The success of this stratagem was further enhanced by his masterful handling of his men. From this time on a general war was inaugurated; Sitting Bull looked to him as a principal war leader, and even the Cheyenne chiefs, allies of the Sioux, practically acknowledged his leadership. Yet during the following ten years of defensive war he was never known to make a speech, though his teepee was the rendezvous of the young men. He was depended upon to put into action the decisions of the council, and was frequently consulted by the older chiefs.

Like Osceola, he rose suddenly; like Tecumseh he was always impatient for battle; like Pontiac, he fought on while his allies were suing for peace, and like Grant, the silent soldier, he was a man of deeds and not of words. He won from Custer and Fetterman and Crook. He won every battle that he undertook, with the exception of one or two occasions when he was surprised in the midst of his women and children, and even then he managed to extricate himself in safety from a difficult position.

Early in the year 1876, his runners brought word from Sitting Bull that all the roving bands would converge upon the upper Tongue River in Montana for summer feasts and conferences. There was conflicting news from the reservation. It was rumored that the army would fight the Sioux to a finish; again, it was said that another commission would be sent out to treat with them.

The Indians came together early in June, and formed a series of encampments stretching out from three to four miles, each band keeping separate camp. On June 17, scouts came in and reported the advance of a large body of troops under General Crook. The council sent Crazy Horse with seven hundred men to meet and attack him. These were nearly all young men, many of them under twenty, the flower of the hostile Sioux. They set out at night so as to steal a march upon the enemy, but within three or four miles of his camp they came unexpectedly upon some of his Crow scouts. There was a hurried exchange of shots; the Crows fled back to Crook's camp, pursued by the Sioux. The soldiers had their warning, and it was impossible to enter the well-protected camp. Again and again Crazy Horse charged with his bravest men, in the attempt to bring the troops into the open, but he succeeded only in drawing their fire. Toward afternoon he withdrew, and returned to camp disappointed. His scouts remained to watch Crook's movements, and later brought word that he had retreated to Goose Creek and seemed to have no further disposition to disturb the Sioux. It is well known to us that it is Crook rather than Reno who is to be blamed for cowardice in connection with Custer's fate. The latter had no chance to do anything, he was lucky to save himself; but if Crook had kept on his way, as ordered, to meet Terry, with his one thousand regulars and two hundred Crow and Shoshone scouts, he would inevitably have intercepted Custer in his advance and saved the day for him, and war with the Sioux would have ended right there. Instead of this, he fell back upon Fort Meade, eating his horses on the way, in a country swarming with game, for fear of Crazy Horse and his braves!

The Indians now crossed the divide between the Tongue and the Little Big Horn, where they felt safe from immediate pursuit. Here, with all their precautions, they were caught unawares by General Custer, in the midst of their midday games and festivities, while many were out upon the daily hunt.

On this twenty-fifth of June, 1876, the great camp was scattered for three miles or more along the level river bottom, back of the thin line of cottonwoods—five circular rows of tee-pees, ranging from half a mile to a mile and a half in circumference. Here and there stood out a large, white, solitary teepee; these were the lodges or "clubs" of the young men. Crazy Horse was a member of the "Strong Hearts" and the "Tokala" or Fox lodge. He was watching a game of ring-toss when the warning came from the southern end of the camp of the approach of troops.

The Sioux and the Cheyennes were "minute men", and although taken by surprise, they instantly responded. Meanwhile, the women and children were thrown into confusion. Dogs were howling, ponies running hither and thither, pursued by their owners, while many of the old men were singing their lodge songs to encourage the warriors, or praising the "strong heart" of Crazy Horse.

That leader had quickly saddled his favorite war pony and was starting with his young men for the south end of the camp, when a fresh alarm came from the opposite direction, and looking up, he saw Custer's force upon the top of the bluff directly across the river. As quick as a flash, he took in the situation—the enemy had planned to attack the camp at both ends at once; and knowing that Custer could not ford the river at that point, he instantly led his men northward to the ford to cut him off. The Cheyennes followed closely. Custer must have seen that wonderful dash up the sage-bush plain, and one wonders whether he realized its meaning. In a very few minutes, this wild general of the plains had outwitted one of the most brilliant leaders of the Civil War and ended at once his military career and his life.

In this dashing charge, Crazy Horse snatched his most famous victory out of what seemed frightful peril, for the Sioux could not know how many were behind Custer. He was caught in his own trap. To the soldiers it must have seemed as if the Indians rose up from the earth to overwhelm them. They closed in from three sides and fought until not a white man was left alive. Then they went down to Reno's stand and found him so well intrenched in a deep gully that it was impossible to dislodge him. Gall and his men held him there until the approach of General Terry compelled the Sioux to break camp and scatter in different directions.

While Sitting Bull was pursued into Canada, Crazy Horse and the Cheyennes wandered about, comparatively undisturbed, during the rest of that year, until in the winter the army surprised the Cheyennes, but did not do them much harm, possibly because they knew that Crazy Horse was not far off. His name was held in wholesome respect. From time to time, delegations of friendly Indians were sent to him, to urge him to come in to the reservation, promising a full hearing and fair treatment.

For some time he held out, but the rapid disappearance of the buffalo, their only means of support, probably weighed with him more than any other influence. In July, 1877, he was finally prevailed upon to come in to Fort Robinson, Nebraska, with several thousand Indians, most of them Ogallala and Minneconwoju Sioux, on the distinct understanding that the government would hear and adjust their grievances.

At this juncture General Crook proclaimed Spotted Tail, who had rendered much valuable service to the army, head chief of the Sioux, which was resented by many. The attention paid Crazy Horse was offensive to Spotted Tail and the Indian scouts, who planned a conspiracy against him. They reported to General Crook that the young chief would murder him at the next council, and stampede the Sioux into another war. He was urged not to attend the council and did not, but sent another officer to represent him. Meanwhile the friends of Crazy Horse discovered the plot and told him of it. His reply was, "Only cowards are murderers."

His wife was critically ill at the time, and he decided to take her to her parents at Spotted Tail agency, whereupon his enemies circulated the story that he had fled, and a party of scouts was sent after him. They overtook him riding with his wife and one other but did not undertake to arrest him, and after he had left the sick woman with her people he went to call on Captain Lea, the agent for the Brulés, accompanied by all the warriors of the Minneconwoju band. This volunteer escort made an imposing appearance on horseback, shouting and singing, and in the words of Captain Lea himself and the missionary, the Reverend Mr. Cleveland, the situation was extremely critical. Indeed, the scouts who had followed Crazy Horse from Red Cloud agency were advised not to show themselves, as some of the warriors had urged that they be taken out and horsewhipped publicly.

Under these circumstances Crazy Horse again showed his masterful spirit by holding these young men in check. He said to them in his quiet way: "It is well to be brave in the field of battle; it is cowardly to display bravery against one's own tribesmen. These scouts have been compelled to do what they did; they are no better than servants of the white officers. I came here on a peaceful errand."

The captain urged him to report at army headquarters to explain himself and correct false rumors, and on his giving consent, furnished him with a wagon and escort. It has been said that he went back under arrest, but this is untrue. Indians have boasted that they had a hand in bringing him in, but their stories are without foundation. He went of his own accord, either suspecting no treachery or determined to defy it.

When he reached the military camp, Little Big Man walked arm-in-arm with him, and his cousin and friend, Touch-the-Cloud, was just in advance. After they passed the sentinel, an officer approached them and walked on his other side. He was unarmed but for the knife which is carried for ordinary uses by women as well as men. Unsuspectingly he walked toward the guardhouse, when Touch-the-Cloud suddenly turned back exclaiming: "Cousin, they will put you in prison!"

"Another white man's trick! Let me go! Let me die fighting!" cried Crazy Horse. He stopped and tried to free himself and draw his knife, but both arms were held fast by Little Big Man and the officer. While he struggled thus, a soldier thrust him through with his bayonet from behind. The wound was mortal, and he died in the course of that night, his old father singing the death song over him and afterward carrying away the body, which they said must not be further polluted by the touch of a white man. They hid it somewhere in the Bad Lands, his resting place to this day.

Thus died one of the ablest and truest American Indians. His life was ideal; his record clean. He was never involved in any of the numerous massacres on the trail, but was a leader in practically every open fight. Such characters as those of Crazy Horse and Chief Joseph are not easily found among so-called civilized people. The reputation of great men is apt to be shadowed by questionable motives and policies, but here are two pure patriots, as worthy of honor as any who ever breathed God's air in the wide spaces of a new world.

Sitting Bull

IT is not easy to characterize Sitting Bull, of all Sioux chiefs most generally known to the American people. There are few to whom his name is not familiar, and still fewer who have learned to connect it with anything more than the conventional notion of a bloodthirsty savage. The man was an enigma at best. He was not impulsive, nor was he phlegmatic. He was most serious when he seemed to be jocose. He was gifted with the power of sarcasm, and few have used it more artfully than he.

His father was one of the best-known members of the Unkpapa band of Sioux. The manner of this man's death was characteristic. One day, when the Unkpapas were attacked by a large war party of Crows, he fell upon the enemy's war leader with his knife. In a hand-to-hand combat of this sort, we count the victor as entitled to a war bonnet of trailing plumes. It means certain death to one or both. In this case, both men dealt a mortal stroke, and Jumping Buffalo, the father of Sitting Bull, fell from his saddle and died in a few minutes. The other died later from the effects of the wound.

Sitting Bull's boyhood must have been a happy one. It was long after the day of the dog-travaux, and his father owned many ponies of variegated colors. It was said of him in a joking way that his legs were bowed like the ribs of the ponies that he rode constantly from childhood. He had also a common nickname that was much to the point. It was "Hunkeshnee", which means "Slow", referring to his inability to run fast, or more probably to the fact that he seldom appeared on foot. In their boyish games he was wont to take the part of the "old man", but this does not mean that he was not active and brave. It is told that after a buffalo hunt the boys were enjoying a mimic hunt with the calves that had been left behind. A large calf turned viciously on Sitting Bull, whose pony had thrown him, but the alert youth got hold of both ears and struggled until the calf was pushed back into a buffalo wallow in a sitting posture. The boys shouted: "He has subdued the buffalo calf! He made it sit down!" And from this incident was derived his familiar name of Sitting Bull.

It is a mistake to suppose that Sitting Bull, or any other Indian warrior, was of a murderous disposition. It is true that savage warfare had grown more and more harsh and cruel since the coming of white traders among them, bringing guns, knives, and whisky. Yet it was still regarded largely as a sort of game, undertaken in order to develop the manly qualities of their youth. It was the degree of risk which brought honor, rather than the number slain, and a brave must mourn thirty days, with blackened face and loosened hair, for the enemy whose life he had taken. While the spoils of war were allowed, this did not extend to territorial aggrandizement, nor was there any wish to overthrow another nation and enslave its people. It was a point of honor in the old days to treat a captive with kindness. The common impression that the Indian is naturally cruel and revengeful is entirely opposed to his philosophy and training. The revengeful tendency of the Indian was aroused by the white man. It is not the natural Indian who is mean and tricky; not Massasoit but King Philip; not Attackullakulla but Weatherford; not Wabashaw but Little Crow; not Jumping Buffalo but Sitting Bull! These men lifted their hands against the white man, while their fathers held theirs out to him with gifts.

Remember that there were councils which gave their decisions in accordance with the highest ideal of human justice before there were any cities on this continent; before there were bridges to span the Mississippi; before this network of railroads was dreamed of! There were primitive communities upon the very spot where Chicago or New York City now stands, where men were as children, innocent of all the crimes now committed there daily and nightly. True morality is more easily maintained in connection with the simple life. You must accept the truth that you demoralize any race whom you have subjugated.

From this point of view we shall consider Sitting Bull's career. We say he is an untutored man: that is true so far as learning of a literary type is concerned; but he was not an untutored man when you view him from the standpoint of his nation. To be sure, he did not learn his lessons from books. This is second-hand information at best. All that he learned he verified for himself and put into daily practice. In personal appearance he was rather commonplace and made no immediate impression, but as he talked he seemed to take hold of his hearers more and more. He was bull-headed; quick to grasp a situation, and not readily induced to change his mind. He was not suspicious until he was forced to be so. All his meaner traits were inevitably developed by the events of his later career.

Sitting Bull's history has been written many times by newspaper men and army officers, but I find no account of him which is entirely correct. I met him personally in 1884, and since his death I have gone thoroughly into the details of his life with his relatives and contemporaries. It has often been said that he was a physical coward and not a warrior. Judge of this for yourselves from the deed which first gave him fame in his own tribe, when he was about twenty-eight years old.

In an attack upon a band of Crow Indians, one of the enemy took his stand, after the rest had fled, in a deep ditch from which it seemed impossible to dislodge him. The situation had already cost the lives of several warriors, but they could not let him go to repeat such a boast over the Sioux!

"Follow me!" said Sitting Bull, and charged. He raced his horse to the brim of the ditch and struck at the enemy with his coup-staff, thus compelling him to expose himself to the fire of the others while shooting his assailant. But the Crow merely poked his empty gun into his face and dodged back under cover. Then Sitting Bull stopped; he saw that no one had followed him, and he also perceived that the enemy had no more ammunition left. He rode deliberately up to the barrier and threw his loaded gun over it; then he went back to his party and told them what he thought of them.

"Now," said he, "I have armed him, for I will not see a brave man killed unarmed. I will strike him again with my coup-staff to count the first feather; who will count the second?" Again he led the charge, and this time they all followed him. Sitting Bull was severely wounded by his own gun in the hands of the enemy, who was killed by those that came after him. This is a record that so far as I know was never made by any other warrior. The second incident that made him well known was his taking of a boy captive in battle with the Assiniboines. He saved this boy's life and adopted him as his brother. Hóhay, as he was called, was devoted to Sitting Bull and helped much in later years to spread his fame. Sitting Bull was a born diplomat, a ready speaker, and in middle life he ceased to go upon the warpath, to become the councilor of his people. From this time on, this man represented him in all important battles, and upon every brave deed done was wont to exclaim aloud:

"I, Sitting Bull's boy, do this in his name!"

He had a nephew, now living, who resembles him strongly, and who also represented him personally upon the field; and so far as there is any remnant left of his immediate band, they look upon this man One Bull as their chief.

When Sitting Bull was a boy, there was no thought of trouble with the whites. He was acquainted with many of the early traders, Picotte, Choteau, Primeau, Larpenteur, and others, and liked them, as did most of his people in those days. All the early records show this friendly attitude of the Sioux, and the great fur companies for a century and a half depended upon them for the bulk of their trade. It was not until the middle of the last century that they woke up all of a sudden to the danger threatening their very existence. Yet at that time many of the old chiefs had been already depraved by the whisky and other vices of the whites, and in the vicinity of the forts and trading posts at Sioux City, Saint Paul, and Cheyenne, there was general demoralization. The drunkards and hangers-on were ready to sell almost anything they had for the favor of the trader. The better and stronger element held aloof. They would not have anything of the white man except his hatchet, gun, and knife. They utterly refused to cede their lands; and as for the rest, they were willing to let him alone as long as he did not interfere with their life and customs, which was not long. It was not, however, the Unkpapa band of Sioux, Sitting Bull's band, which first took up arms against the whites; and this was not because they had come less in contact with them, for they dwelt on the Missouri River, the natural highway of trade. As early as 1854, the Ogallalas and Brulés had trouble with the soldiers near Fort Laramie; and again in 1857 Inkpaduta massacred several families of settlers at Spirit Lake, Iowa. Finally, in 1862, the Minnesota Sioux, goaded by many wrongs, arose and murdered many of the settlers, afterward fleeing into the country of the Unkpapas and appealing to them for help, urging that all Indians should make common cause against the invader. This brought Sitting Bull face to face with a question which was not yet fully matured in his own mind; but having satisfied himself of the justice of their cause, he joined forces with the renegades during the summer of 1863, and from this time on he was an acknowledged leader.

In 1865 and 1866 he met the Canadian half-breed, Louis Riel, instigator of two rebellions, who had come across the line for safety; and in fact at this time he harbored a number of outlaws and fugitives from justice. His conversations with these, especially with the French mixed-bloods, who inflamed his prejudices against the Americans, all had their influence in making of the wily Sioux a determined enemy to the white man. While among his own people he was always affable and genial, he became boastful and domineering in his dealings with the hated race. He once remarked that "if we wish to make any impression upon the pale-face, it is necessary to put on his mask."

Sitting Bull joined in the attack on Fort Phil Kearny and in the subsequent hostilities; but he accepted in good faith the treaty of 1868, and soon after it was signed he visited Washington with Red Cloud and Spotted Tail, on which occasion the three distinguished chiefs attracted much attention and were entertained at dinner by President Grant and other notables. He considered that the life of the white man as he saw it was no life for his people, but hoped by close adherence to the terms of this treaty to preserve the Big Horn and Black Hills country for a permanent hunting ground. When gold was discovered and the irrepressible gold seekers made their historic dash across the plains into this forbidden paradise, then his faith in the white man's honor was gone forever, and he took his final and most persistent stand in defense of his nation and home. His bitter and at the same time well-grounded and philosophical dislike of the conquering race is well expressed in a speech made before the purely Indian council before referred to, upon the Powder River. I will give it in brief as it has been several times repeated to me by men who were present.

"Behold, my friends, the spring is come; the earth has gladly received the embraces of the sun, and we shall soon see the results of their love! Every seed is awakened, and all animal life. It is through this mysterious power that we too have our being, and we therefore yield to our neighbors, even to our animal neighbors, the same right as ourselves to inhabit this vast land.

"Yet hear me, friends! we have now to deal with another people, small and feeble when our forefathers first met with them, but now great and overbearing. Strangely enough, they have a mind to till the soil, and the love of possessions is a disease in them. These people have made many rules that the rich may break, but the poor may not! They have a religion in which the poor worship, but the rich will not! They even take tithes of the poor and weak to support the rich and those who rule. They claim this mother of ours, the Earth, for their own use, and fence their neighbors away from her, and deface her with their buildings and their refuse. They compel her to produce out of season, and when sterile she is made to take medicine in order to produce again. All this is sacrilege.

"This nation is like a spring freshet; it overruns its banks and destroys all who are in its path. We cannot dwell side by side. Only seven years ago we made a treaty by which we were assured that the buffalo country should be left to us forever. Now they threaten to take that from us also. My brothers, shall we submit? or shall we say to them: 'First kill me, before you can take possession of my fatherland!' "

As Sitting Bull spoke, so he felt, and he had the courage to stand by his words. Crazy Horse led his forces in the field; as for him, he applied his energies to state affairs, and by his strong and aggressive personality contributed much to holding the hostiles together.

It may be said without fear of contradiction that Sitting Bull never killed any women or children. He was a fair fighter, and while not prominent in battle after his young manhood, he was the brains of the Sioux resistance. He has been called a "medicine man" and a "dreamer." Strictly speaking, he was neither of these, and the white historians are prone to confuse the two. A medicine man is a doctor or healer; a dreamer is an active war prophet who leads his war party according to his dream or prophecy. What is called by whites "making medicine" in war time is again a wrong conception. Every warrior carries a bag of sacred or lucky charms, supposed to protect the wearer alone, but it has nothing to do with the success or safety of the party as a whole. No one can make any "medicine" to affect the result of a battle, although it has been said that Sitting Bull did this at the battle of the Little Big Horn.

When Custer and Reno attacked the camp at both ends, the chief was caught napping. The village was in danger of surprise, and the women and children must be placed in safety. Like other men of his age, Sitting Bull got his family together for flight, and then joined the warriors on the Reno side of the attack. Thus he was not in the famous charge against Custer; nevertheless, his voice was heard exhorting the warriors throughout that day.

During the autumn of 1876, after the fall of Custer, Sitting Bull was hunted all through the Yellowstone region by the military. The following characteristic letter, doubtless written at his dictation by a half-breed interpreter, was sent to Colonel Otis immediately after a daring attack upon his wagon train.

"I want to know what you are doing, traveling on this road. You scare all the buffalo away. I want to hunt in this place. I want you to turn back from here. If you don't, I will fight you again. I want you to leave what you have got here and turn back from here.

> I am your friend
> Sitting Bull.

I mean all the rations you have got and some powder. Wish you would write me as soon as you can."

Otis, however, kept on and joined Colonel Miles, who followed Sitting Bull with about four hundred soldiers. He overtook him at last on Cedar Creek, near the Yellowstone, and the two met midway between the lines for a parley. The army report says: "Sitting Bull wanted peace in his own way." The truth was that he wanted nothing more than had been guaranteed to them by the treaty of 1868—the exclusive possession of their last hunting ground. This the government was not now prepared to grant, as it had been decided to place all the Indians under military control upon the various reservations.

Since it was impossible to reconcile two such conflicting demands, the hostiles were driven about from pillar to post for several more years, and finally took refuge across the line in Canada, where Sitting Bull had placed his last hope of justice and freedom for his race. Here he was joined from time to time by parties of malcontents from the reservation, driven largely by starvation and ill-treatment to seek another home. Here, too, they were followed by United States commissioners, headed by General Terry, who endeavored to persuade him to return, promising abundance of food and fair treatment, despite the fact that the exiles were well aware of the miserable condition of the "good Indians" upon the reservations. He first refused to meet them at all, and only did so when advised to that effect by Major Walsh of the Canadian mounted police. This was his characteristic remark: "If you have one honest man in Washington, send him here and I will talk to him."

Sitting Bull was not moved by fair words; but when he found that if they had liberty on that side, they had little else, that the Canadian government would give them protection but no food; that the buffalo had been all but exterminated and his starving people were already beginning to desert him, he was compelled at last, in 1881, to report at Fort Buford, North Dakota, with his band of hungry, homeless, and discouraged refugees. It was, after all, to hunger and not to the strong arm of the military that he surrendered in the end.

In spite of the invitation that had been extended to him in the name of the "Great Father" at Washington, he was immediately thrown into a military prison, and afterward handed over to Colonel Cody ("Buffalo Bill") as an advertisement for his "Wild West Show." After traveling about for several years with the famous showman, thus increasing his knowledge of the weaknesses as well as the strength of the white man, the deposed and humiliated chief settled down quietly with his people upon the Standing Rock agency in North Dakota, where his immediate band occupied the Grand River district and set to raising cattle and horses. They made good progress; much better, in fact, than that of the "coffee-coolers" or "loafer" Indians, received the missionaries kindly and were soon a church-going people.

When the Commissions of 1888 and 1889 came to treat with the Sioux for a further cession of land and a reduction of their reservations, nearly all were opposed to consent on any terms. Nevertheless, by hook or by crook, enough signatures were finally obtained to carry the measure through, although it is said that many were those of women and the so-called "squaw-men", who had no rights in the land. At the same time, rations were cut down, and there was general hardship and dissatisfaction. Crazy Horse was long since dead; Spotted Tail had fallen at the hands of one of his own tribe; Red Cloud had become a feeble old man, and the disaffected among the Sioux began once more to look to Sitting Bull for leadership.

At this crisis a strange thing happened. A half-breed Indian in Nevada promulgated the news that the Messiah had appeared to him upon a peak in the Rockies, dressed in rabbit skins, and bringing a message to the red race. The message was to the effect that since his first coming had been in vain, since the white people had doubted and reviled him, had nailed him to the cross, and trampled upon his doctrines, he had come again in pity to save the Indian. He declared that he would cause the earth to shake and to overthrow the cities of the whites and destroy them, that the buffalo would return, and the land belong to the red race forever! These events were to come to pass within two years; and meanwhile they were to prepare for his coming by the ceremonies and dances which he commanded.

This curious story spread like wildfire and met with eager

acceptance among the suffering and discontented people. The teachings of Christian missionaries had prepared them to believe in a Messiah, and the prescribed ceremonial was much more in accord with their traditions than the conventional worship of the churches. Chiefs of many tribes sent delegations to the Indian prophet; Short Bull, Kicking Bear, and others went from among the Sioux, and on their return all inaugurated the dances at once. There was an attempt at first to keep the matter secret, but it soon became generally known and seriously disconcerted the Indian agents and others, who were quick to suspect a hostile conspiracy under all this religious enthusiasm. As a matter of fact, there was no thought of an uprising; the dancing was innocent enough, and pathetic enough their despairing hope in a pitiful Saviour who should overwhelm their oppressors and bring back their golden age.

When the Indians refused to give up the "Ghost Dance" at the bidding of the authorities, the growing suspicion and alarm focused upon Sitting Bull, who in spirit had never been any too submissive, and it was determined to order his arrest. At the special request of Major McLaughlin, agent at Standing Rock, forty of his Indian police were sent out to Sitting Bull's home on Grand River to secure his person (followed at some little distance by a body of United States troops for reinforcement, in case of trouble). These police are enlisted from among the tribesmen at each agency, and have proved uniformly brave and faithful. They entered the cabin at daybreak, aroused the chief from a sound slumber, helped him to dress, and led him unresisting from the house; but when he came out in the gray dawn of that December morning in 1890, to find his cabin surrounded by armed men and himself led away to he knew not what fate, he cried out loudly:

"They have taken me: what say you to it?"

Men poured out of the neighboring houses, and in a few minutes the police were themselves surrounded with an excited and rapidly increasing throng. They harangued the crowd in vain; Sitting Bull's blood was up, and he again appealed to his men. His adopted brother, the Assiniboine captive whose life he had saved so many years before, was the first to fire. His shot killed Lieutenant Bull Head, who held Sitting Bull by the arm. Then there was a short but sharp conflict, in which Sitting Bull and six of his defenders and six of the Indian police were slain, with many more wounded. The chief's young son, Crow Foot, and his devoted "brother" died with him. When all was over, and the terrified people had fled precipitately across the river, the soldiers appeared upon the brow of the long hill and fired their Hotchkiss guns into the deserted camp.

Thus ended the life of a natural strategist of no mean courage and ability. The great chief was buried without honors outside the cemetery at the post, and for some years the grave was marked by a mere board at its head. Recently some women have built a cairn of rocks there in token of respect and remembrance.

Red Cloud

Charles Eastman (Ohiyesa)

Little Crow

Spotted Tail

Sitting Bull

Gall

Two Strike

Rain-in-the-Face

American Horse

Dull Knife

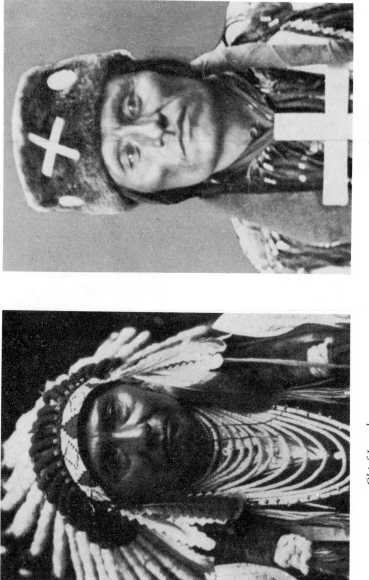

Little Wolf

Chief Joseph

Rain-in-the-Face

THE noted Sioux warrior, Rain-in-the-Face, whose name once carried terror to every part of the frontier, died at his home on the Standing Rock reserve in North Dakota on September 14, 1905. About two months before his death I went to see him for the last time, where he lay upon the bed of sickness from which he never rose again, and drew from him his life-history.

It had been my experience that you cannot induce an Indian to tell a story, or even his own name, by asking him directly.

"Friend," I said, "even if a man is on a hot trail, he stops for a smoke! In the good old days, before the charge there was a smoke. At home, by the fireside, when the old men were asked to tell their brave deeds, again the pipe was passed. So come, let us smoke now to the memory of the old days!"

He took of my tobacco and filled his long pipe, and we smoked. Then I told an old mirthful story to get him in the humor of relating his own history.

The old man lay upon an iron bedstead, covered by a red blanket, in a corner of the little log cabin. He was all alone that day; only an old dog lay silent and watchful at his master's feet.

Finally he looked up and said with a pleasant smile:

"True, friend; it is the old custom to retrace one's trail before leaving it forever! I know that I am at the door of the spirit home.

"I was born near the forks of the Cheyenne River, about seventy years ago. My father was not a chief; my grandfather was not a chief, but a good hunter and a feast-maker. On my mother's side I had some noted ancestors, but they left me no chieftainship. I had to work for my reputation.

"When I was a boy, I loved to fight," he continued. "In all our boyish games I had the name of being hard to handle, and I took much pride in the fact.

"I was about ten years old when we encountered a band of Cheyennes. They were on friendly terms with us, but we boys always indulged in sham fights on such occasions, and this time I got in an honest fight with a Cheyenne boy older than I. I got the best of the boy, but he hit me hard in the face several times, and my face was all spattered with blood and streaked where the paint had been washed away. The Sioux boys whooped and yelled:

" 'His enemy is down, and his face is spattered as if with rain! Rain-in-the-Face! His name shall be Rain-in-the-Face!'

"Afterwards, when I was a young man, we went on a warpath against the Gros Ventres. We stole some of their horses, but were overtaken and had to abandon the horses and fight for our lives. I had wished my face to represent the sun when partly covered with darkness, so I painted it half black, half red. We fought all day in the rain, and my face was partly washed and streaked with red and black: so again I was christened Rain-in-the-Face. We considered it an honorable name.

"I had been on many warpaths, but was not especially successful until about the time the Sioux began to fight with the white man. One of the most daring attacks that we ever made was at Fort Totten, North Dakota, in the summer of 1866.

"Hóhay, the Assiniboine captive of Sitting Bull, was the leader in this raid. Wapáypay, the Fearless Bear, who was afterward hanged at Yankton, was the bravest man among us. He dared Hóhay to make the charge. Hóhay accepted the challenge, and in turn dared the other to ride with him through the agency and right under the walls of the fort, which was well garrisoned and strong.

"Wapáypay and I in those days called each other 'brother-friend.' It was a life-and-death vow. What one does the other must do; and that meant that I must be in the forefront of the charge, and if he is killed, I must fight until I die also!

"I prepared for death. I painted as usual like an eclipse of the sun, half black and half red."

His eyes gleamed and his face lighted up remarkably as he

talked, pushing his black hair back from his forehead with a nervous gesture.

"Now the signal for the charge was given! I started even with Wapáypay, but his horse was faster than mine, so he left me a little behind as we neared the fort. This was bad for me, for by that time the soldiers had somewhat recovered from the surprise and were aiming better.

"Their big gun talked very loud, but my Wapáypay was leading on, leaning forward on his fleet pony like a flying squirrel on a smooth log! He held his rawhide shield on the right side, a little to the front, and so did I. Our warwhoop was like the coyotes singing in the evening, when they smell blood!

"The soldiers' guns talked fast, but few were hurt. Their big gun was like a toothless old dog, who only makes himself hotter the more noise he makes," he remarked with some humor.

"How much harm we did I do not know, but we made things lively for a time; and the white men acted as people do when a swarm of angry bees get into camp. We made a successful retreat, but some of the reservation Indians followed us yelling, until Hóhay told them that he did not wish to fight with the captives of the white man, for there would be no honor in that. There was blood running down my leg, and I found that both my horse and I were slightly wounded.

"Some two years later we attacked a fort west of the Black Hills [Fort Phil Kearny, Wyoming]. It was there we killed one hundred soldiers." [The military reports say eighty men, under the command of Captain Fetterman—not one left alive to tell the tale!] "Nearly every band of the Sioux nation was represented in that fight—Red Cloud, Spotted Tail, Crazy Horse, Sitting Bull, Big Foot, and all our great chiefs were there. Of course such men as I were then comparatively unknown. However, there were many noted young warriors, among them Sword, the younger Young-Man-Afraid, American Horse [afterward chief], Crow King, and others.

"This was the plan decided upon after many councils. The main war party lay in ambush, and a few of the bravest young men were appointed to attack the wood-choppers who were cutting logs to complete the building of the fort. We were told not to kill these men, but to chase them into the fort and retreat slowly, defying the white men; and if the soldiers should follow, we were to lead them into the ambush. They took our bait exactly as we had hoped! It was a matter of a very few minutes, for every soldier lay dead in a shorter time than it takes to annihilate a small herd of buffalo.

"This attack was hastened because most of the Sioux on the Missouri River and eastward had begun to talk of suing for peace. But even this did not stop the peace movement. The very next year a treaty was signed at Fort Rice, Dakota Territory, by nearly all the Sioux chiefs, in which it was agreed on the part of the Great Father in Washington that all the country north of the Republican River in Nebraska, including the Black Hills and the Big Horn Mountains, was to be always Sioux country, and no white man should intrude upon it without our permission. Even with this agreement Sitting Bull and Crazy Horse were not satisfied, and they would not sign.

"Up to this time I had fought in some important battles, but had achieved no great deed. I was ambitious to make a name for myself. I joined war parties against the Crows, Mandans, Gros Ventres, and Pawnees, and gained some little distinction.

"It was when the white men found the yellow metal in our country, and came in great numbers, driving away our game, that we took up arms against them for the last time. I must say here that the chiefs who were loudest for war were among the first to submit and accept reservation life. Spotted Tail was a great warrior, yet he was one of the first to yield, because he was promised by the Chief Soldiers that they would make him chief of all the Sioux. Ugh! he would have stayed with Sitting Bull to the last had it not been for his ambition.

"About this time we young warriors began to watch the trails of the white men into the Black Hills, and when we saw a wagon coming we would hide at the crossing and kill them all without much trouble. We did this to discourage the whites from coming into our country without our permission. It was the duty of our Great Father at Washington, by the agreement of 1868, to keep his white children away.

"During the troublesome time after this treaty, which no one seemed to respect, either white or Indian [but the whites broke it first], I was like many other young men—much on the warpath, but with little honor. I had not yet become noted for any great deed. Finally, Wapáypay and I waylaid and killed a white soldier on his way from the fort to his home in the east.

"There were a few Indians who were liars, and never on the warpath, playing 'good Indian' with the Indian agents and the war chiefs at the forts. Some of this faithless set betrayed me, and told more than I ever did. I was seized and taken to the fort near Bismarck, North Dakota [Fort Abraham Lincoln], by a brother [Tom Custer] of the Long-Haired War Chief, and imprisoned there. These same lying Indians, who were selling their services as scouts to the white man, told me that I was to be shot to death, or else hanged upon a tree. I answered that I was not afraid to die.

"However, there was an old soldier who used to bring my food and stand guard over me—he was a white man, it is true, but he had an Indian heart! He came to me one day and unfastened the iron chain and ball with which they had locked my leg, saying by signs and what little Sioux he could muster:

"'Go, friend! take the chain and ball with you. I shall shoot, but the voice of the gun will lie.'

"When he had made me understand, you may guess that I ran my best! I was almost over the bank when he fired his piece at me several times, but I had already gained cover and was safe. I have never told this before, and would not, lest it should do him an injury, but he was an old man then, and I am sure he must be dead long since. That old soldier taught me that some of the white people have hearts," he added, quite seriously.

"I went back to Standing Rock in the night, and I had to hide for several days in the woods, where food was brought to me by my relatives. The Indian police were ordered to retake me, and they pretended to hunt for me, but really they did not, for if they had found me I would have died with one or two of them, and they knew it! In a few days I departed with several others, and we rejoined the hostile camp on the Powder River and made some trouble for the men who were building the great iron track north of us [Northern Pacific].

"In the spring the hostile Sioux got together again upon the

Tongue River. It was one of the greatest camps of the Sioux that I ever saw. There were some Northern Cheyennes with us, under Two Moon, and a few Santee Sioux, renegades from Canada, under Inkpaduta, who had killed white people in Iowa long before. We had decided to fight the white soldiers until no warrior should be left."

At this point Rain-in-the-Face took up his tobacco pouch and began again to fill his pipe.

"Of course the younger warriors were delighted with the prospect of a great fight! Our scouts had discovered piles of oats for horses and other supplies near the Missouri River. They had been brought by the white man's fire-boats. Presently they reported a great army about a day's travel to the south, with Shoshone and Crow scouts.

"There was excitement among the people, and a great council was held. Many spoke. I was asked the condition of those Indians who had gone upon the reservation, and I told them truly that they were nothing more than prisoners. It was decided to go out and meet Three Stars [General Crook] at a safe distance from our camp.

"We met him on the Little Rosebud. I believe that if we had waited and allowed him to make the attack, he would have fared no better than Custer. He was too strongly fortified where he was, and I think, too, that he was saved partly by his Indian allies, for the scouts discovered us first and fought us first, thus giving him time to make his preparations. I think he was more wise than brave! After we had left that neighborhood he might have pushed on and connected with the Long-Haired Chief. That would have saved Custer and perhaps won the day.

"When we crossed from Tongue River to the Little Big Horn, on account of the scarcity of game, we did not anticipate any more trouble. Our runners had discovered that Crook had retraced his trail to Goose Creek, and we did not suppose that the white men would care to follow us farther into the rough country.

"Suddenly the Long-Haired Chief appeared with his men! It was a surprise."

"What part of the camp were you in when the soldiers attacked the lower end?" I asked.

"I had been invited to a feast at one of the young men's lodges [a sort of club]. There was a certain warrior who was making preparations to go against the Crows, and I had decided to go also," he said.

"While I was eating my meat we heard the war cry! We all rushed out, and saw a warrior riding at top speed from the lower camp, giving the warning as he came. Then we heard the reports of the soldiers' guns, which sounded differently from the guns fired by our people in battle.

"I ran to my teepee and seized my gun, a bow, and a quiver full of arrows. I already had my stone war club, for you know we usually carry those by way of ornament. Just as I was about to set out to meet Reno, a body of soldiers appeared nearly opposite us, at the edge of a long line of cliffs across the river.

"All of us who were mounted and ready immediately started down the stream toward the fort. There were Ogallalas, Minneconjous, Cheyennes, and some Unkpapas, and those around me seemed to be nearly all very young men.

" 'Behold, there is among us a young woman!' I shouted. 'Let no young man hide behind her garment!' I knew that would make those young men brave.

"The woman was Tashenamani, or Moving Robe, whose brother had just been killed in the fight with Three Stars. Holding her brother's war staff over her head, and leaning forward upon her charger, she looked as pretty as a bird. Always when there is a woman in the charge, it causes the warriors to vie with one another in displaying their valor," he added.

"The foremost warriors had almost surrounded the white men, and more were continually crossing the stream. The soldiers had dismounted, and were firing into the camp from the top of the cliff."

"My friend, was Sitting Bull in this fight?" I inquired.

"I did not see him there, but I learned afterward that he was among those who met Reno, and that was three or four of the white man's miles from Custer's position. Later he joined the attack upon Custer, but was not among the foremost.

"When the troops were surrounded on two sides, with the river on the third, the order came to charge! There were many very

young men, some of whom had only a war staff or a stone war
club in hand, who plunged into the column, knocking the men
over and stampeding their horses.

"The soldiers had mounted and started back, but when the onset came they dismounted again and separated into several divisions, facing different ways. They fired as fast as they could load
their guns, while we used chiefly arrows and war clubs. There
seemed to be two distinct movements among the Indians. One
body moved continually in a circle, while the other rode directly
into and through the troops.

"Presently some of the soldiers remounted and fled along the
ridge toward Reno's position; but they were followed by our warriors, like hundreds of blackbirds after a hawk. A larger body
remained together at the upper end of a little ravine, and fought
bravely until they were cut to pieces. I had always thought that
white men were cowards, but I had a great respect for them after
this day.

"It is generally said that a young man with nothing but a war
staff in his hand broke through the column and knocked down the
leader very early in the fight. We supposed him to be the leader,
because he stood up in full view, swinging his big knife [sword]
over his head, and talking loud. Some one unknown afterwards
shot the chief, and he was probably killed also; for if not, he
would have told of the deed, and called others to witness it. So it
is that no one knows who killed the Long-Haired Chief [General
Custer].

"After the first rush was over, *coups* were counted as usual on
the bodies of the slain. You know four *coups* [or blows] can be
counted on the body of an enemy, and whoever counts the first
one [touches it for the first time] is entitled to the 'first feather.'

"There was an Indian here called Appearing Elk, who died a
short time ago. He was slightly wounded in the charge. He had
some of the weapons of the Long-Haired Chief, and the Indians
used to say jokingly after we came upon the reservation that
Appearing Elk must have killed the Chief, because he had his
sword! However, the scramble for plunder did not begin until all
were dead. I do not think he killed Custer, and if he had, the time
to claim the honor was immediately after the fight.

"Many lies have been told of me. Some say that I killed the Chief, and others that I cut out the heart of his brother [Tom Custer], because he had caused me to be imprisoned. Why, in that fight the excitement was so great that we scarcely recognized our nearest friends! Everything was done like lightning. After the battle we young men were chasing horses all over the prairie, while the old men and women plundered the bodies; and if any mutilating was done, it was by the old men.

"I have lived peaceably ever since we came upon the reservation. No one can say that Rain-in-the-Face has broken the rules of the Great Father. I fought for my people and my country. When we were conquered I remained silent, as a warrior should. Rain-in-the-Face was killed when he put down his weapons before the Great Father. His spirit was gone then; only his poor body lived on, but now it is almost ready to lie down for the last time. Ho, hechetu! [It is well.]"

Two Strike

IT is a pity that so many interesting names of well-known Indians have been mistranslated, so that their meaning becomes very vague if it is not wholly lost. In some cases an opposite meaning is conveyed. For instance there is the name, "Young-Man-Afraid-of-His-Horses." It does not mean that the owner of the name is afraid of his own horse—far from it! Tashunkekokipapi signifies "The young men [of the enemy] fear his horses." Whenever that man attacks, the enemy knows there will be a determined charge.

The name Tashunkewitko, or Crazy Horse, is a poetic simile. This leader was likened to an untrained or untouched horse, wild, ignorant of domestic uses, splendid in action, and unconscious of danger.

The name of Two Strike is a deed name. In a battle with the Utes this man knocked two enemies from the back of a war horse. The true rendering of the name Nomkahpa would be, "He knocked off two."

I was well acquainted with Two Strike and spent many pleasant hours with him, both at Washington, D. C., and in his home on the Rosebud reservation. What I have written is not all taken from his own mouth, because he was modest in talking about himself, but I had him vouch for the truth of the stories. He said that he was born near the Republican River about 1832. His earliest recollection was of an attack by the Shoshones upon their camp on the Little Piney. The first white men he ever met were traders who visited his people when he was very young. The incident was still vividly with him, because, he said, "They made my father collected ponies, fine robes, and other acceptable goods to be given away in honor of the event, whenever it should take place. Now and then they would drop a sly hint, but with no perceptible effect.

They did not and could not know of the inward struggle that racked his mind at this period of his life. The shy and modest young man was dying for a wife, yet could not bear even to think of speaking to a young woman! The fearless hunter of buffaloes, mountain lions, and grizzlies, the youth who had won his eagle feathers in a battle with the Utes, could not bring himself to take this tremendous step.

At last his father appealed to him directly. "My son," he declared, "it is your duty to take unto yourself a wife, in order that the honors won by your ancestors and by yourself may be handed down in the direct line. There are several eligible young women in our band whose parents have intimated a wish to have you for their son-in-law."

Two Strike made no reply, but he was greatly disturbed. He had no wish to have the old folks select his bride, for if the truth were told, his choice was already made. He had simply lacked the courage to go a-courting!

The next morning, after making an unusually careful toilet, he took his best horse and rode to a point overlooking the path by which the girls went for water. Here the young men were wont to take their stand, and, if fortunate, intercept the girl of their heart for a brief but fateful interview. Two Strike had determined to speak straight to the point, and as soon as he saw the pretty maid he came forward boldly and placed himself in her way. A long moment passed. She glanced up at him shyly but not without encouragement. His teeth fairly chattered with fright, and he could not say a word. She looked again, noted his strange looks, and believed him suddenly taken ill. He appeared to be suffering. At last he feebly made signs for her to go on and leave him alone. The maiden was sympathetic, but as she did not know what else to do she obeyed his request.

The poor youth was so ashamed of his cowardice that he afterward admitted his first thought was to take his own life. He believed he had disgraced himself forever in the eyes of the only

crazy" [drunk]. This made a deep impression upon him, he told me, so that from that day he was always afraid of the white man's "mysterious water."

Two Strike was not a large man, but he was very supple and alert in motion, as agile as an antelope. His face was mobile and intelligent. Although he had the usual somber visage of an Indian, his expression brightened up wonderfully when he talked. In some ways wily and shrewd in intellect, he was not deceitful nor mean. He had a high sense of duty and honor. Patriotism was his ideal and goal of life.

As a young man he was modest and even shy, although both his father and grandfather were well-known chiefs. I could find few noteworthy incidents in his early life, save that he was an expert rider of wild horses. At one time I was pressing him to give me some interesting incident of his boyhood. He replied to the effect that there was plenty of excitement but "not much in it." There was a delegation of Sioux chiefs visiting Washington, and we were spending an evening together in their hotel. Hollow Horn Bear spoke up and said:

"Why don't you tell him how you and a buffalo cow together held your poor father up and froze him almost to death?"

Everybody laughed, and another man remarked: "I think he had better tell the medicine man (meaning myself) how he lost the power of speech when he first tried to court a girl." Two Strike, although he was then close to eighty years of age, was visibly embarrassed by their chaff.

"Anyway, I stuck to the trail. I kept on till I got what I wanted," he muttered. And then came the story.

The old chief, his father, was very fond of the buffalo hunt; and being accomplished in horsemanship and a fine shot, although not very powerfully built, young Two Strike was already following hard in his footsteps. Like every proud father, his was giving him every incentive to perfect his skill, and one day challenged his sixteen-year-old son to the feat of "one arrow to kill" at the very next chase.

It was midwinter. A large herd of buffalo was reported by the game scout. The hunters gathered at daybreak prepared for the charge. The old chief had his tried charger equipped with a soft, pillow-like Indian saddle and a lariat. His old sinew-backed hickory bow was examined and strung, and a fine straight arrow with a steel head carefully selected for the test. He adjusted a keen butcher knife over his leather belt, which held a warm buffalo robe securely about his body. He wore neither shirt nor coat, although a piercing wind was blowing from the northwest. The youthful Two Strike had his favorite bow and his swift pony, which was perhaps dearer to him than his closest boy comrade.

Now the hunters crouched upon their horses' necks like an army in line of battle, while behind them waited the boys and old men with pack ponies to carry the meat. "Hukahey!" shouted the leader as a warning. "Yekiya wo!" (Go) and in an instant all the ponies leaped forward against the cutting wind, as if it were the start in a horse race. Every rider leaned forward, tightly wrapped in his robe, watching the flying herd for an opening in the mass of buffalo, a chance to cut out some of the fattest cows. This was the object of the race.

The chief had a fair start; his horse was well trained and needed no urging nor guidance. Without the slightest pull on the lariat he dashed into the thickest of the herd. The youth's pony had been prancing and rearing impatiently; he started a little behind, yet being swift passed many. His rider had one clear glimpse of his father ahead of him, then the snow arose in blinding clouds on the trail of the bison. The whoops of the hunters, the lowing of the cows, and the menacing glances of the bulls as they plunged along, or now and then stood at bay, were enough to unnerve a boy less well tried. He was unable to select his victim. He had been carried deeply into the midst of the herd and found himself helpless to make the one sure shot, therefore he held his one arrow in his mouth and merely strove to separate them so as to get his chance.

At last the herd parted, and he cut out two fat cows, and was maneuvering for position when a rider appeared out of the snow cloud on their other side. This aroused him to make haste lest his rival secure both cows; he saw his chance, and in a twinkling his arrow sped clear through one of the animals so that she fell headlong.

In this instant he observed that the man who had joined him

was his own father, who had met with the same difficulties as himself. When the young man had shot his only arrow, the old chief with a whoop went after the cow that was left, but as he gained her broadside, his horse stepped in a badger hole and fell, throwing him headlong. The maddened buffalo, as sometimes happens in such cases, turned upon the pony and gored him to death. His rider lay motionless, while Two Strike rushed forward to draw her attention, but she merely tossed her head at him, while persistently standing guard over the dead horse and the all but frozen Indian.

Alas for the game of "one arrow to kill!" The boy must think fast, for his father's robe had slipped off, and he was playing dead, lying almost naked in the bitter air upon the trampled snow. His bluff would not serve, so he flew back to pull out his solitary arrow from the body of the dead cow. Quickly wheeling again, he sent it into her side and she fell. The one arrow to kill had become one arrow to kill two buffalo! At the council lodge that evening Two Strike was the hero.

The following story is equally characteristic of him, and in explanation it should be said that in the good old days among the Sioux, a young man is not supposed to associate with girls until he is ready to take a wife. It was a rule with our young men, especially the honorable and well-born, to gain some reputation in the hunt and in war,—the more difficult the feats achieved the better,—before even speaking to a young woman. Many a life was risked in the effort to establish a reputation along these lines. Courtship was no secret, but rather a social event, often celebrated by the proud parents with feasts and presents to the poor, and this etiquette was sometimes felt by a shy or sensitive youth as an insurmountable obstacle to the fulfilment of his desires.

Two Strike was the son and grandson of a chief, but he could not claim any credit for the deeds of his forbears. He had not only to guard their good name but achieve one for himself. This he had set out to do, and he did well. He was now of marriageable age with a war record, and admitted to the council, yet he did not seem to trouble himself at all about a wife. His was strictly a bachelor career. Meanwhile, as is apt to be the case, his parents had thought much about a possible daughter-in-law, and had even girl he had ever loved. However, he determined to conquer his weakness and win her, which he did. The story came out many years after and was told with much enjoyment by the old men.

Two Strike was better known by his own people than by the whites, for he was individually a terror in battle rather than a leader. He achieved his honorable name in a skirmish with the Utes in Colorado. The Sioux regarded these people as their bravest enemies, and the outcome of the fight was for some time uncertain. First the Sioux were forced to retreat and then their opponents, and at the latter point the horse of a certain Ute was shot under him. A friend came to his rescue and took him up behind him. Our hero overtook them in flight, raised his war club, and knocked both men off with one blow.

He was a very old man when he died, only two or three years ago, on the Rosebud reservation.

American Horse

ONE of the wittiest and shrewdest of the Sioux chiefs was American Horse, who succeeded to the name and position of an uncle, killed in the battle of Slim Buttes in 1876. The younger American Horse was born a little before the encroachments of the whites upon the Sioux country became serious and their methods aggressive, and his early manhood brought him into that most trying and critical period of our history. He had been tutored by his uncle, since his own father was killed in battle while he was still very young. The American Horse band was closely attached to a trading post, and its members in consequence were inclined to be friendly with the whites, a policy closely adhered to by their leader.

When he was born, his old grandfather said: "Put him out in the sun! Let him ask his great-grandfather, the Sun, for the warm blood of a warrior!" And he had warm blood. He was a genial man, liking notoriety and excitement. He always seized an opportunity to leap into the center of the arena.

In early life he was a clownish sort of boy among the boys—an expert mimic and impersonator. This talent made him popular and in his way a leader. He was a natural actor, and early showed marked ability as a speaker.

American Horse was about ten years old when he was attacked by three Crow warriors, while driving a herd of ponies to water. Here he displayed native cunning and initiative. It seemed he had scarcely a chance to escape, for the enemy was near. He yelled frantically at the ponies to start them toward home, while he dropped off into a thicket of willows and hid there. A part of the herd was caught in sight of the camp and there was a counter chase, but the Crows got away with the ponies. Of course his mother was frantic, believing her boy had been killed or captured; but after the excitement was over, he appeared in camp unhurt. When questioned about his escape, he remarked: "I knew they would not take the time to hunt for small game when there was so much bigger close by."

When he was quite a big boy, he joined in a buffalo hunt, and on the way back with the rest of the hunters his mule became unmanageable. American Horse had insisted on riding him in addition to a heavy load of meat and skins, and the animal evidently resented this, for he suddenly began to run and kick, scattering fresh meat along the road, to the merriment of the crowd. But the boy turned actor, and made it appear that it was at his wish the mule had given this diverting performance. He clung to the back of his plunging and braying mount like a circus rider, singing a Brave Heart song, and finally brought up amid the laughter and cheers of his companions. Far from admitting defeat, he boasted of his horsemanship and declared that his "brother" the donkey would put any enemy to flight, and that they should be called upon to lead a charge.

It was several years later that he went to sleep early one night and slept soundly, having been scouting for two nights previous. It happened that there was a raid by the Crows, and when he awoke in the midst of the yelling and confusion, he sprang up and attempted to join in the fighting. Everybody knew his voice in all the din, so when he fired his gun and announced a coup, as was the custom, others rushed to the spot, to find that he had shot a hobbled pony belonging to their own camp. The laugh was on him, and he never recovered from his chagrin at this mistake. In fact, although he was undoubtedly fearless and tried hard to distinguish himself in warfare, he did not succeed.

It is told of him that he once went with a war party of young men to the Wind River country against the Shoshones. At last they discovered a large camp, but there were only a dozen or so of the Sioux, therefore they hid themselves and watched for their opportunity to attack an isolated party of hunters. While waiting thus, they ran short of food. One day a small party of Shoshones was seen near at hand, and in the midst of the excitement and preparations for the attack, young American Horse caught sight of a fat black-tail deer close by. Unable to resist the temptation, he pulled an arrow from his quiver and sent it through the deer's heart, then with several of his half-starved companions sprang upon the yet quivering body of the animal to cut out the liver, which was sometimes eaten raw. One of the men was knocked down, it is said, by the last kick of the dying buck, but having swallowed a few mouthfuls the warriors rushed upon and routed their enemies. It is still told of American Horse how he killed game and feasted between the ambush and the attack.

At another time he was drying his sacred war bonnet and other gear over a small fire. These articles were held in great veneration by the Indians and handled accordingly. Suddenly the fire blazed up, and our hero so far forgot himself as to begin energetically beating out the flames with the war bonnet, breaking off one of the sacred buffalo horns in the act. One could almost fill a book with his mishaps and exploits. I will give one of them in his own words as well as I can remember them.

"We were as promising a party of young warriors as our tribe ever sent against any of its ancestral enemies. It was mid-summer, and after going two days' journey from home we began to send two scouts ahead daily while the main body kept a half day behind. The scouts set out every evening and traveled all night. One night the great war pipe was held out to me and to Young-Man-Afraid-of-His-Horses. At daybreak, having met no one, we hid our horses and climbed to the top of the nearest butte to take an observation. It was a very hot day. We lay flat on our blankets, facing the west where the cliff fell off in a sheer descent, and with our backs toward the more gradual slope dotted with scrub pines and cedars. We stuck some tall grass on our heads and proceeded to study the landscape spread before us for any sign of man.

"The sweeping valleys were dotted with herds, both large and small, of buffalo and elk, and now and then we caught a glimpse of a coyote slinking into the gulches, returning from night hunting to sleep. While intently watching some moving body at a distance, we could not yet tell whether of men or animals, I heard a faint noise behind me and slowly turned my head. Behold! a grizzly bear sneaking up on all fours and almost ready to spring! " 'Run!' I yelled into the ear of my companion, and we both leaped to our feet in a second. 'Separate! separate!' he shouted, and as we did so, the bear chose me for his meat. I ran downhill as fast as I could, but he was gaining. 'Dodge around a tree!' screamed Young-Man-Afraid. I took a deep breath and made a last spurt, desperately circling the first tree I came to. As the ground was steep just there, I turned a somersault one way and the bear the other. I picked myself up in time to climb the tree, and was fairly out of reach when he gathered himself together and came at me more furiously than ever, holding in one paw the shreds of my breechcloth, for in the fall he had just scratched my back and cut my belt in two, and carried off my only garment for a trophy!

"My friend was well up another tree and laughing heartily at my predicament, and when the bear saw that he could not get at either of us he reluctantly departed, after I had politely addressed him and promised to make an offering to his spirit on my safe return. I don't think I ever had a narrower escape," he concluded.

During the troublous times from 1865 to 1877, American Horse advocated yielding to the government at any cost, being no doubt convinced of the uselessness of resistance. He was not a recognized leader until 1876, when he took the name and place of his uncle. Up to this time he bore the nickname of Manishnee (Can not walk, or Played out.)

When the greater part of the Ogallalas, to which band he belonged, came into the reservation, he at once allied himself with the peace element at the Red Cloud agency, near Fort Robinson, Nebraska, and took no small part in keeping the young braves quiet. Since the older and better-known chiefs, with the exception of Spotted Tail, were believed to be hostile at heart, the military made much use of him. Many of his young men enlisted as scouts by his advice, and even he himself entered the service.

In the early part of the year 1876, there was a rumor that certain bands were in danger of breaking away. Their leader was one Sioux Jim, so nicknamed by the soldiers. American Horse went to him as peacemaker, but was told he was a woman and no brave.

He returned to his own camp and told his men that Sioux Jim meant mischief, and in order to prevent another calamity to the tribe, he must be chastised. He again approached the war-like Jim with several warriors at his back. The recalcitrant came out, gun in hand, but the wily chief was too quick for him. He shot and wounded the rebel, whereupon one of his men came forward and killed him.

This quelled the people for the time being and up to the killing of Crazy Horse. In the crisis precipitated by this event, American Horse was again influential and energetic in the cause of the government. From this time on he became an active participant in the affairs of the Teton Sioux. He was noted for his eloquence, which was nearly always conciliatory, yet he could say very sharp things of the duplicity of the whites. He had much ease of manner and was a master of repartee. I recall his saying that if you have got to wear golden slippers to enter the white man's heaven no Indian will ever get there, as the whites have got the Black Hills and with them all the gold.

It was during the last struggle of his people, at the time of the Messiah craze in 1890–1891, that he demonstrated as never before the real greatness of the man. While many of his friends were carried away by the new thought, he held aloof from it and cautioned his band to do the same. When it developed into an extensive upheaval among the nations he took his positive stand against it.

Presently all Indians who did not dance the Ghost Dance were ordered to come into camp at Pine Ridge agency. American Horse was the first to bring in his people. I was there at the time and talked with him daily. When Little was arrested, it had been agreed among the disaffected to have him resist, which meant that he would be roughly handled. This was to be their excuse to attack the Indian police, which would probably lead to a general massacre or outbreak. I know that this desperate move was opposed from the beginning by American Horse, and it was believed that his life was threatened.

On the day of the "Big Issue", when thousands of Indians were gathered at the agency, this man Little, who had been in hiding, walked boldly among them. Of course the police would arrest him at sight, and he was led toward the guardhouse. He struggled with them, but was overpowered. A crowd of warriors rushed to his rescue, and there was confusion and a general shout of "Hurry up with them! Kill them all!" I saw American Horse walk out of the agent's office and calmly face the excited mob.

"What are you going to do?" he asked. "Stop, men, stop and think before you act! Will you murder your children, your women, yes, destroy your nation to-day?" He stood before them like a statue and the men who held the two policemen helpless paused for an instant. He went on: "You are brave to-day because you outnumber the white men, but what will you do to-morrow? There are railroads on all sides of you. The soldiers will pour in from every direction by thousands and surround you. You have little food or ammunition. It will be the end of your people. Stop, I say, stop now!"

Jack Red Cloud, son of the old chief, rushed up to him and thrust a revolver almost in his face. "It is you and men like you," he shouted, "who have reduced our race to slavery and starvation!" American Horse did not flinch but deliberately re-entered the office, followed by Jack still flourishing the pistol. But his timely appearance and eloquence had saved the day. Others of the police force had time to reach the spot, and with a large crowd of friendly Indians had taken command of the situation.

When I went into the office I found him alone but apparently quite calm. "Where are the agent and the clerks?" I asked. "They fled by the back door," he replied, smiling. "I think they are in the cellar. These fools outside had almost caught us asleep, but I think it is over now."

American Horse was one of the earliest advocates of education for the Indian, and his son Samuel and nephew Robert were among the first students at Carlisle. I think one or two of his daughters were the handsomest Indian girls of full blood that I ever saw. His record as a councilor of his people and his policy in the new situation that confronted them was manly and consistent.

Dull Knife

THE life of Dull Knife, the Cheyenne, is a true hero tale. Simple, childlike yet manful, and devoid of selfish aims, or love of gain, he is a pattern for heroes of any race.

Dull Knife was a chief of the old school. Among all the Indians of the plains, nothing counts save proven worth. A man's caliber is measured by his courage, unselfishness and intelligence. Many writers confuse history with fiction, but in Indian history their women and old men and even children witness the main events, and not being absorbed in daily papers and magazines, these events are rehearsed over and over with few variations. Though orally preserved, their accounts are therefore accurate. But they have seldom been willing to give reliable information to strangers, especially when asked and paid for.

Racial prejudice naturally enters into the account of a man's life by enemy writers, while one is likely to favor his own race. I am conscious that many readers may think that I have idealized the Indian. Therefore I will confess now that we have too many weak and unprincipled men among us. When I speak of the Indian hero, I do not forget the mongrel in spirit, false to the ideals of his people. Our trustfulness has been our weakness, and when the vices of civilization were added to our own, we fell heavily.

It is said that Dull Knife as a boy was resourceful and self-reliant. He was only nine years old when his family was separated from the rest of the tribe while on a buffalo hunt. His father was away and his mother busy, and he was playing with his little sister on the banks of a stream, when a large herd of buffalo swept down upon them on a stampede for water. His mother climbed a tree, but the little boy led his sister into an old beaver house whose entrance was above water, and here they remained in shelter until the buffalo passed and they were found by their distracted parents.

Dull Knife was quite a youth when his tribe was caught one winter in a region devoid of game, and threatened with starvation. The situation was made worse by heavy storms, but he secured help and led a relief party a hundred and fifty miles, carrying bales of dried buffalo meat on pack horses.

Another exploit that made him dear to his people occurred in battle, when his brother-in-law was severely wounded and left lying where no one on either side dared to approach him. As soon as Dull Knife heard of it he got on a fresh horse, and made so daring a charge that others joined him; thus under cover of their fire he rescued his brother-in-law, and in so doing was wounded twice.

The Sioux knew him as a man of high type, perhaps not so brilliant as Roman Nose and Two Moon, but surpassing both in honesty and simplicity, as well as in his war record. (Two Moon, in fact, was never a leader of his people, and became distinguished only in wars with the whites during the period of revolt.) A story is told of an ancestor of the same name that illustrates well the spirit of the age.

It was the custom in those days for the older men to walk ahead of the moving caravan and decide upon all halts and camping places. One day the councilors came to a grove of wild cherries covered with ripe fruit, and they stopped at once. Suddenly a grizzly charged from the thicket. The men yelped and hooted, but the bear was not to be bluffed. He knocked down the first warrior who dared to face him and dragged his victim into the bushes.

The whole caravan was in the wildest excitement. Several of the swiftest-footed warriors charged the bear, to bring him out into the open, while the women and dogs made all the noise they could. The bear accepted the challenge, and as he did so, the man whom they had supposed dead came running from the opposite end of the thicket. The Indians were delighted, and especially so when in the midst of their cheers, the man stopped running for his life and began to sing a Brave Heart song as he approached the grove with his butcher knife in his hand. He would dare his enemy again!

The grizzly met him with a tremendous rush, and they went down together. Instantly the bear began to utter cries of distress, and at the same time the knife flashed, and he rolled over dead. The warrior was too quick for the animal; he first bit his sensitive nose to distract his attention, and then used the knife to stab him to the heart. He fought many battles with knives thereafter and claimed that the spirit of the bear gave him success. On one occasion, however, the enemy had a strong buffalo-hide shield which the Cheyenne bear fighter could not pierce through, and he was wounded; nevertheless he managed to dispatch his foe. It was from this incident that he received the name of Dull Knife, which was handed down to his descendant.

As is well known, the Northern Cheyennes uncompromisingly supported the Sioux in their desperate defense of the Black Hills and Big Horn country. Why not? It was their last buffalo region—their subsistence. It was what our wheat fields are to a civilized nation.

About the year 1875, a propaganda was started for confining all the Indians upon reservations, where they would be practically interned or imprisoned, regardless of their possessions and rights. The men who were the strongest advocates of the scheme generally wanted the Indians' property—the one main cause back of all Indian wars. From the warlike Apaches to the peaceful Nez Perces, all the tribes of the plains were hunted from place to place; then the government resorted to peace negotiations, but always with an army at hand to coerce. Once disarmed and helpless, they were to be taken under military guard to the Indian Territory.

A few resisted, and declared they would fight to the death rather than go. Among these were the Sioux, but nearly all the smaller tribes were deported against their wishes. Of course those Indians who came from a mountainous and cold country suffered severely. The moist heat and malaria decimated the exiles. Chief Joseph of the Nez Perces and Chief Standing Bear of the Poncas appealed to the people of the United States, and finally succeeded in having their bands or the remnant of them returned to their own part of the country. Dull Knife was not successful in his plea, and the story of his flight is one of poignant interest.

He was regarded by the authorities as a dangerous man, and with his depleted band was taken to the Indian Territory without his consent in 1876. When he realized that his people were dying like sheep, he was deeply moved. He called them together. Every man and woman declared that they would rather die in their own country than stay there longer, and they resolved to flee to their northern homes.

Here again was displayed the genius of these people. From the Indian Territory to Dakota is no short dash for freedom. They knew what they were facing. Their line of flight lay through a settled country and they would be closely pursued by the army. No sooner had they started than the telegraph wires sang one song: "The panther of the Cheyennes is at large. Not a child or a woman in Kansas or Nebraska is safe." Yet they evaded all the pursuing and intercepting troops and reached their native soil. The strain was terrible, the hardship great, and Dull Knife, like Joseph, was remarkable for his self-restraint in sparing those who came within his power on the way.

But fate was against him, for there were those looking for blood money who betrayed him when he thought he was among friends. His people were tired out and famished when they were surrounded and taken to Fort Robinson. There the men were put in prison, and their wives guarded in camp. They were allowed to visit their men on certain days. Many of them had lost everything; there were but a few who had even one child left. They were heartbroken.

These despairing women appealed to their husbands to die fighting: their liberty was gone, their homes broken up, and only slavery and gradual extinction in sight. At last Dull Knife listened. He said: "I have lived my life. I am ready." The others agreed. "If our women are willing to die with us, who is there to say no? If we are to do the deeds of men, it rests with you women to bring us our weapons."

As they had been allowed to carry moccasins and other things to the men, so they contrived to take in some guns and knives under this disguise. The plan was to kill the sentinels and run to the nearest natural trench, there to make their last stand. The women and children were to join them. This arrangement was carried out. Not every brave had a gun, but all had agreed to die together. They fought till their small store of ammunition was exhausted, then exposed their broad chests for a target, and the mothers even held up their little ones to be shot. Thus died the fighting Cheyennes and their dauntless leader.

Roman Nose

THIS Cheyenne war chief was a contemporary of Dull Knife. He was not so strong a character as the other, and was inclined to be pompous and boastful; but with all this he was a true type of native American in spirit and bravery.

While Dull Knife was noted in warfare among Indians, Roman Nose made his record against the whites, in defense of territory embracing the Republican and Arickaree rivers. He was killed on the latter river in 1868, in the celebrated battle with General Forsythe.

Save Chief Gall and Washakie in the prime of their manhood, this chief had no peer in bodily perfection and masterful personality. No Greek or Roman gymnast was ever a finer model of physical beauty and power. He thrilled his men to frenzied action when he came upon the field. It was said of him that he sacrificed more youths by his personal influence in battle than any other leader, being very reckless himself in grand-stand charges. He was killed needlessly in this manner.

Roman Nose always rode an uncommonly fine, spirited horse, and with his war bonnet and other paraphernalia gave a wonderful exhibition. The Indians used to say that the soldiers must gaze at him rather than aim at him, as they so seldom hit him even when running the gantlet before a firing line.

He did a remarkable thing once when on a one-arrow-to-kill buffalo hunt with his brother-in-law. His companion had selected his animal and drew so powerfully on his sinew bowstring that it broke. Roman Nose had killed his own cow and was whipping up close to the other when the misfortune occurred. Both horses were going at full speed and the arrow jerked up in the air. Roman Nose caught it and shot the cow for him.

Another curious story told of him is to the effect that he had an intimate Sioux friend who was courting a Cheyenne girl, but without success. As the wooing of both Sioux and Cheyennes was pretty much all effected in the night time, Roman Nose told his friend to let him do the courting for him. He arranged with the young woman to elope the next night and to spend the honeymoon among his Sioux friends. He then told his friend what to do. The Sioux followed instructions and carried off the Cheyenne maid, and not until morning did she discover her mistake. It is said she never admitted it, and that the two lived happily together to a good old age, so perhaps there was no mistake after all.

Perhaps no other chief attacked more emigrants going west on the Oregon Trail between 1860 and 1868. He once made an attack on a large party of Mormons, and in this instance the Mormons had time to form a corral with their wagons and shelter their women, children, and horses. The men stood outside and met the Indians with well-aimed volleys, but they circled the wagons with whirlwind speed, and whenever a white man fell, it was the signal for Roman Nose to charge and count the "coup." The hat of one of the dead men was off, and although he had heavy hair and beard, the top of his head was bald from the forehead up. As custom required such a deed to be announced on the spot, the chief yelled at the top of his voice:

"Your Roman Nose has counted the first coup on the longest-faced white man who was ever killed!"

When the Northern Cheyennes under this daring leader attacked a body of scouting troops under the brilliant officer General Forsythe, Roman Nose thought that he had a comparatively easy task. The first onset failed, and the command entrenched itself on a little island. The wily chief thought he could stampede them and urged on his braves with the declaration that the first to reach the island should be entitled to wear a trailing war bonnet. Nevertheless he was disappointed, and his men received such a warm reception that none succeeded in reaching it. In order to inspire them to desperate deeds he had led them in person, and with him that meant victory or death. According to the army accounts, it was a thrilling moment, and might well have proved disastrous to the Forsythe command, whose leader was wounded and helpless. The danger was acute until Roman Nose fell, and even then his lieutenants were bent upon crossing at any cost, but some of the older chiefs prevailed upon them to withdraw.

Thus the brilliant war chief of the Cheyennes came to his death. If he had lived until 1876, Sitting Bull would have had another bold ally.

Chief Joseph

THE Nez Perce tribe of Indians, like other tribes too large to be united under one chief, was composed of several bands, each distinct in sovereignty. It was a loose confederacy. Joseph and his people occupied the Imnaha or Grande Ronde valley in Oregon, which was considered perhaps the finest land in that part of the country.

When the last treaty was entered into by some of the bands of the Nez Perce, Joseph's band was at Lapwai, Idaho, and had nothing to do with the agreement. The elder chief in dying had counseled his son, then not more than twenty-two or twenty-three years of age, never to part with their home, assuring him that he had signed no papers. These peaceful non-treaty Indians did not even know what land had been ceded until the agent read them the government order to leave. Of course they refused. You and I would have done the same.

When the agent failed to move them, he and the would-be settlers called upon the army to force them to be good, namely, without a murmur to leave their pleasant inheritance in the hands of a crowd of greedy grafters. General O. O. Howard, the Christian soldier, was sent to do the work.

He had a long council with Joseph and his leading men, telling them they must obey the order or be driven out by force. We may be sure that he presented this hard alternative reluctantly. Joseph was a mere youth without experience in war or public affairs. He had been well brought up in obedience to parental wisdom and with his brother Ollicut had attended Missionary Spaulding's school where they had listened to the story of Christ and his religion of brotherhood. He now replied in his simple way that neither he nor his father had ever made any treaty disposing of their country, that no other band of the Nez Perces was authorized to speak for them, and it would seem a mighty injustice and unkindness to dispossess a friendly band.

General Howard told them in effect that they had no rights, no voice in the matter: they had only to obey. Although some of the lesser chiefs counseled revolt then and there, Joseph maintained his self-control, seeking to calm his people, and still groping for a peaceful settlement of their difficulties. He finally asked for thirty days' time in which to find and dispose of their stock, and this was granted.

Joseph steadfastly held his immediate followers to their promise, but the land-grabbers were impatient, and did everything in their power to bring about an immediate crisis so as to hasten the eviction of the Indians. Depredations were committed, and finally the Indians, or some of them, retaliated, which was just what their enemies had been looking for. There might be a score of white men murdered among themselves on the frontier and no outsider would ever hear about it, but if one were injured by an Indian—"Down with the bloodthirsty savages!" was the cry.

Joseph told me himself that during all of those thirty days a tremendous pressure was brought upon him by his own people to resist the government order. "The worst of it was," said he, "that everything they said was true; besides"—he paused for a moment—"it seemed very soon for me to forget my father's dying words, 'Do not give up our home!' " Knowing as I do just what this would mean to an Indian, I felt for him deeply.

Among the opposition leaders were Too-hul-hul-sote, White Bird, and Looking Glass, all of them strong men and respected by the Indians; while on the other side were men built up by emissaries of the government for their own purposes and advertised as "great friendly chiefs." As a rule such men are unworthy, and this is so well known to the Indians that it makes them distrustful of the government's sincerity at the start. Moreover, while Indians unqualifiedly say what they mean, the whites have a hundred ways of saying what they do not mean.

The center of the storm was this simple young man, who so far as I can learn had never been upon the warpath, and he stood firm for peace and obedience. As for his father's sacred dying charge, he told himself that he would not sign any papers, he would not go of his free will but from compulsion, and this was his excuse.

However, the whites were unduly impatient to clear the coveted valley, and by their insolence they aggravated to the danger point an already strained situation. The murder of an Indian was the climax, and this happened in the absence of the young chief. He returned to find the leaders determined to die fighting. The nature of the country was in their favor and at least they could give the army a chase, but how long they could hold out they did not know. Even Joseph's younger brother Ollicut was won over. There was nothing for him to do but fight; and then and there began the peaceful Joseph's career as a general of unsurpassed strategy in conducting one of the most masterly retreats in history.

This is not my judgment, but the unbiased opinion of men whose knowledge and experience fit them to render it. Bear in mind that these people were not scalp hunters like the Sioux, Cheyennes, and Utes, but peaceful hunters and fishermen. The first council of war was a strange business to Joseph. He had only this to say to his people:

"I have tried to save you from suffering and sorrow. Resistance means all of that. We are few. They are many. You can see all we have at a glance. They have food and ammunition in abundance. We must suffer great hardship and loss." After this speech, he quietly began his plans for the defense.

The main plan of campaign was to engineer a successful retreat into Montana and there form a junction with the hostile Sioux and Cheyennes under Sitting Bull. There was a relay scouting system, one set of scouts leaving the main body at evening and the second a little before daybreak, passing the first set on some commanding hill top. There were also decoy scouts set to trap Indian scouts of the army. I notice that General Howard charges his Crow scouts with being unfaithful.

Their greatest difficulty was in meeting an unencumbered army, while carrying their women, children, and old men, with supplies and such household effects as were absolutely necessary. Joseph formed an auxiliary corps that was to effect a retreat at each engagement, upon a definite plan and in definite order, while the unencumbered women were made into an ambulance corps to take care of the wounded.

It was decided that the main rear guard should meet General Howard's command in White Bird Canyon, and every detail was planned in advance, yet left flexible according to Indian custom, giving each leader freedom to act according to circumstances. Perhaps no better ambush was ever planned than the one Chief Joseph set for the shrewd and experienced General Howard. He expected to be hotly pursued, but he calculated that the pursuing force would consist of not more than two hundred and fifty soldiers. He prepared false trails to mislead them into thinking that he was about to cross or had crossed the Salmon River, which he had not thought of doing at that time. Some of the tents were pitched in plain sight, while the women and children were hidden on the inaccessible ridges, and the men concealed in the canyon ready to fire upon the soldiers with deadly effect with scarcely any danger to themselves. They could even roll rocks upon them.

In a very few minutes the troops had learned a lesson. The soldiers showed some fight, but a large body of frontiersmen who accompanied them were soon in disorder. The warriors chased them nearly ten miles, securing rifles and much ammunition, and killing and wounding many.

The Nez Percés next crossed the river, made a detour and recrossed it at another point, then took their way eastward. All this was by way of delaying pursuit. Joseph told me that he estimated it would take six or seven days to get a sufficient force in the field to take up their trail, and the correctness of his reasoning is apparent from the facts as detailed in General Howard's book. He tells us that he waited six days for the arrival of men from various forts in his department, then followed Joseph with six hundred soldiers, beside a large number of citizen volunteers and his Indian scouts. As it was evident they had a long chase over trackless wilderness in prospect, he discarded his supply wagons and took pack mules instead. But by this time the Indians had a good start.

Meanwhile General Howard had sent a dispatch to Colonel Gibbons, with orders to head Joseph off, which he undertook to do at the Montana end of the Lolo Trail. The wily commander had no knowledge of this move, but he was not to be surprised. He was too brainy for his pursuers, whom he constantly outwitted, and only gave battle when he was ready. There at the Big Hole Pass he met Colonel Gibbons' fresh troops and pressed them close. He sent a party under his brother Ollicut to harass Gibbons' rear and rout the pack mules, thus throwing him on the defensive and causing him to send for help, while Joseph continued his masterly retreat toward the Yellowstone Park, then a wilderness. However, this was but little advantage to him, since he must necessarily leave a broad trail, and the army was augmenting its columns day by day with celebrated scouts, both white and Indian. The two commands came together, and although General Howard says their horses were by this time worn out, and by inference the men as well, they persisted on the trail of a party encumbered by women and children, the old, sick, and wounded.

It was decided to send a detachment of cavalry under Bacon, to Tash Pass, the gateway of the National Park, which Joseph would have to pass, with orders to detain him there until the rest could come up with them. Here is what General Howard says of the affair. "Bacon got into position soon enough but he did not have the heart to fight the Indians on account of their number." Meanwhile another incident had occurred. Right under the eyes of the chosen scouts and vigilant sentinels, Joseph's warriors fired upon the army camp at night and ran off their mules. He went straight on toward the park, where Lieutenant Bacon let him get by and pass through the narrow gateway without firing a shot.

Here again it was demonstrated that General Howard could not depend upon the volunteers, many of whom had joined him in the chase, and were going to show the soldiers how to fight Indians. In this night attack at Camas Meadow, they were demoralized, and while crossing the river next day many lost their guns in the water, whereupon all packed up and went home, leaving the army to be guided by the Indian scouts.

However, this succession of defeats did not discourage General Howard, who kept on with as many of his men as were able to carry a gun, meanwhile sending dispatches to all the frontier posts with orders to intercept Joseph if possible. Sturgis tried to stop him as the Indians entered the Park, but they did not meet until he was about to come out, when there was another fight, with Joseph again victorious. General Howard came upon the battle field soon afterward and saw that the Indians were off again, and from here he sent fresh messages to General Miles, asking for reinforcements.

Joseph had now turned northeastward toward the Upper Missouri. He told me that when he got into that part of the country he knew he was very near the Canadian line and could not be far from Sitting Bull, with whom he desired to form an alliance. He also believed that he had cleared all the forts. Therefore he went more slowly and tried to give his people some rest. Some of their best men had been killed or wounded in battle, and the wounded were a great burden to him; nevertheless they were carried and tended patiently all during this wonderful flight. Not one was ever left behind.

It is the general belief that Indians are cruel and revengeful, and surely these people had reason to hate the race who had driven them from their homes if any people ever had. Yet it is a fact that when Joseph met visitors and travelers in the Park, some of whom were women, he allowed them to pass unharmed, and in at least one instance let them have horses. He told me that he gave strict orders to his men not to kill any women or children. He wished to meet his adversaries according to their own standards of warfare, but he afterward learned that in spite of professions of humanity, white soldiers have not seldom been known to kill women and children indiscriminately.

Another remarkable thing about this noted retreat is that Joseph's people stood behind him to a man, and even the women and little boys did each his part. The latter were used as scouts in the immediate vicinity of the camp.

The Bittersweet valley, which they had now entered, was full of game, and the Indians hunted for food, while resting their worn-out ponies. One morning they had a council to which Joseph rode over bareback, as they had camped in two divisions a little apart. His fifteen-year-old daughter went with him. They discussed sending runners to Sitting Bull to ascertain his exact whereabouts and whether it would be agreeable to him to join forces with the Nez Perces. In the midst of the council, a force of United States cavalry charged down the hill between the two camps. This once Joseph was surprised. He had seen no trace of the soldiers and had somewhat relaxed his vigilance.

He told his little daughter to stay where she was, and himself cut right through the cavalry and rode up to his own teepee, where his wife met him at the door with his rifle, crying: "Here is your gun, husband!" The warriors quickly gathered and pressed the soldiers so hard that they had to withdraw. Meanwhile one set of the people fled while Joseph's own band intrenched themselves in a very favorable position from which they could not easily be dislodged.

General Miles had received and acted on General Howard's message, and he now sent one of his officers with some Indian scouts into Joseph's camp to negotiate with the chief. Meantime Howard and Sturgis came up with the encampment, and Howard had with him two friendly Nez Perce scouts who were directed to talk to Joseph in his own language. He decided that there was nothing to do but surrender.

He had believed that his escape was all but secure: then at the last moment he was surprised and caught at a disadvantage. His army was shattered; he had lost most of the leaders in these various fights; his people, including children, women, and the wounded, had traveled thirteen hundred miles in about fifty days, and he himself a young man who had never before taken any important responsibility! Even now he was not actually conquered. He was well intrenched; his people were willing to die fighting; but the army of the United States offered peace and he agreed, as he said, out of pity for his suffering people. Some of his warriors still refused to surrender and slipped out of the camp at night and through the lines. Joseph had, as he told me, between three and four hundred fighting men in the beginning, which means over one thousand persons, and of these several hundred surrendered with him.

His own story of the conditions he made was prepared by himself with my help in 1897, when he came to Washington to present his grievances. I sat up with him nearly all of one night; and I may add here that we took the document to General Miles who was then stationed in Washington, before presenting it to the Department. The General said that every word of it was true.

In the first place, his people were to be kept at Fort Keogh, Montana, over the winter and then returned to their reservation. Instead they were taken to Fort Leavenworth, Kansas, and placed between a lagoon and the Missouri River, where the sanitary conditions made havoc with them. Those who did not die were then taken to the Indian Territory, where the health situation was even worse. Joseph appealed to the government again and again, and at last by the help of Bishops Whipple and Hare he was moved to the Colville reservation in Washington. Here the land was very poor, unlike their own fertile valley. General Miles said to the chief that he had recommended and urged that their agreement be kept, but the politicians and the people who occupied the Indians' land declared they were afraid if he returned he would break out again and murder innocent white settlers! What irony!

The great Chief Joseph died broken-spirited and broken-hearted. He did not hate the whites, for there was nothing small about him, and when he laid down his weapons he would not fight on with his mind. But he was profoundly disappointed in the claims of a Christian civilization. I call him great because he was simple and honest. Without education or special training he demonstrated his ability to lead and to fight when justice demanded. He outgeneraled the best and most experienced commanders in the army of the United States, although their troops were well provisioned, well armed, and above all unencumbered. He was great finally, because he never boasted of his remarkable feat. I am proud of him, because he was a true American.

Little Wolf

IF any people ever fought for liberty and justice, it was the Cheyennes. If any ever demonstrated their physical and moral courage beyond cavil, it was this race of purely American heroes, among whom Little Wolf was a leader.

I knew the chief personally very well. As a young doctor, I was sent to the Pine Ridge agency in 1890, as government physician to the Sioux and the Northern Cheyennes. While I heard from his own lips of that gallant dash of his people from their southern exile to their northern home, I prefer that Americans should read of it in Doctor George Bird Grinnell's book, "The Fighting Cheyennes." No account could be clearer or simpler; and then too, the author cannot be charged with a bias in favor of his own race.

At the time that I knew him, Little Wolf was a handsome man, with the native dignity and gentleness, musical voice, and pleasant address of so many brave leaders of his people. One day when he was dining with us at our home on the reservation, I asked him, as I had a habit of doing, for some reminiscences of his early life. He was rather reluctant to speak, but a friend who was present contributed the following:

"Perhaps I can tell you why it is that he has been a lucky man all his life. When quite a small boy, the tribe was one winter in want of food, and his good mother had saved a small piece of buffalo meat, which she solemnly brought forth and placed before him with the remark: 'My son must be patient, for when he grows up he will know even harder times than this.'

"He had eaten nothing all day and was pretty hungry, but before he could lay hands on the meat a starving dog snatched it and bolted from the teepee. The mother ran after the dog and brought him back for punishment. She tied him to a post and was about to whip him when the boy interfered. 'Don't hurt him, mother!' he cried; 'he took the meat because he was hungrier than I am!' "

I was told of another kind act of his under trying circumstances. While still a youth, he was caught out with a party of buffalo hunters in a blinding blizzard. They were compelled to lie down side by side in the snowdrifts, and it was a day and a night before they could get out. The weather turned very cold, and when the men arose they were in danger of freezing. Little Wolf pressed his fine buffalo robe upon an old man who was shaking with a chill and himself took the other's thin blanket.

As a full-grown young man, he was attracted by a maiden of his tribe, and according to the custom then in vogue the pair disappeared. When they returned to the camp as man and wife, behold! there was great excitement over the affair. It seemed that a certain chief had given many presents and paid unmistakable court to the maid with the intention of marrying her, and her parents had accepted the presents, which meant consent so far as they were concerned. But the girl herself had not given consent.

The resentment of the disappointed suitor was great. It was reported in the village that he had openly declared that the young man who defied and insulted him must expect to be punished. As soon as Little Wolf heard of the threats, he told his father and friends that he had done only what it is every man's privilege to do.

"Tell the chief," said he, "to come out with any weapon he pleases, and I will meet him within the circle of lodges. He shall either do this or eat his words. The woman is not his. Her people accepted his gifts against her wishes. Her heart is mine."

The chief apologized, and thus avoided the inevitable duel, which would have been a fight to the death.

The early life of Little Wolf offered many examples of the dashing bravery characteristic of the Cheyennes, and inspired the younger men to win laurels for themselves. He was still a young man, perhaps thirty-five, when the most trying crisis in the history of his people came upon them. As I know and as Doctor Grinnell's book amply corroborates, he was the general who largely guided and defended them in that tragic flight from the Indian Territory to their northern home. I will not discuss the justice of their cause: I prefer to quote Doctor Grinnell, lest it appear that I am in any way exaggerating the facts.

"They had come," he writes, "from the high, dry country of Montana and North Dakota to the hot and humid Indian Territory. They had come from a country where buffalo and other game were still plentiful to a land where the game had been exterminated. Immediately on their arrival they were attacked by fever and ague, a disease wholly new to them. Food was scanty, and they began to starve. The agent testified before a committee of the Senate that he never received supplies to subsist the Indians for more than nine months in each year. These people were meat-eaters, but the beef furnished them by the government inspectors was no more than skin and bone. The agent in describing their sufferings said: 'They have lived and that is about all.'

"The Indians endured this for about a year, and then their patience gave out. They left the agency to which they had been sent and started north. Though troops were camped close to them, they attempted no concealment of their purpose. Instead, they openly announced that they intended to return to their own country.

"We have heard much in past years of the march of the Nez Perces under Chief Joseph, but little is remembered of the Dull Knife outbreak and the march to the north led by Little Wolf. The story of the journey has not been told, but in the traditions of the old army this campaign was notable, and old men who were stationed on the plains forty years ago are apt to tell you, if you ask them, that there never was such another journey since the Greeks marched to the sea. . . .

"The fugitives pressed constantly northward undaunted, while orders were flying over the wires, and special trains were carrying men and horses to cut them off at all probable points on the different railway lines they must cross. Of the three hundred Indians, sixty or seventy were fighting men—the rest old men, women, and children. An army officer once told me that thirteen thousand troops were hurrying over the country to capture or kill these few poor people who had left the fever-stricken South, and in the face of every obstacle were steadily marching northward.

"The War Department set all its resources in operation against them, yet they kept on. If troops attacked them, they stopped and fought until they had driven off the soldiers, and then started north again. Sometimes they did not even stop, but marched along, fighting as they marched. For the most part they tried—and with success—to avoid conflicts, and had but four real hard fights, in which they lost half a dozen men killed and about as many wounded."

It must not be overlooked that the appeal to justice had first been tried before taking this desperate step. Little Wolf had gone to the agent about the middle of the summer and said to him: "This is not a good country for us, and we wish to return to our home in the mountains where we were always well. If you have not the power to give permission, let some of us go to Washington and tell them there how it is, or do you write to Washington and get permission for us to go back."

"Stay one more year," replied the agent, "and then we will see what we can do for you." "No," said Little Wolf. "Before another year there will be none left to travel north. We must go now."

Soon after this it was found that three of the Indians had disappeared and the chief was ordered to surrender ten men as hostages for their return. He refused. "Three men," said he, "who are traveling over wild country can hide so that they cannot be found. You would never get back these three, and you would keep my men prisoners always."

The agent then threatened if the ten men were not given up to withhold their rations and starve the entire tribe into submission. He forgot that he was addressing a Cheyenne. These people had not understood that they were prisoners when they agreed to friendly relations with the government and came upon the reservation. Little Wolf stood up and shook hands with all present before making his final deliberate address.

"Listen, my friends, I am a friend of the white people and have been so for a long time. I do not want to see blood spilt about this agency. I am going north to my own country. If you are going to send your soldiers after me, I wish you would let us get a little distance away. Then if you want to fight, I will fight you, and we can make the ground bloody at that place."

The Cheyenne was not bluffing. He said just what he meant, and I presume the agent took the hint, for although the military were there they did not undertake to prevent the Indians' departure. Next morning the teepees were pulled down early and quickly. Toward evening of the second day, the scouts signaled the approach of troops. Little Wolf called his men together and advised them under no circumstances to fire until fired upon. An Arapahoe scout was sent to them with a message. "If you surrender now, you will get your rations and be well treated." After what they had endured, it was impossible not to hear such a promise with contempt. Said Little Wolf: "We are going back to our own country. We do not want to fight." He was riding still nearer when the soldiers fired, and at a signal the Cheyennes made a charge. They succeeded in holding off the troops for two days, with only five men wounded and none killed, and when the military retreated the Indians continued northward carrying their wounded.

This sort of thing was repeated again and again. Meanwhile Little Wolf held his men under perfect control. There were practically no depredations. They secured some boxes of ammunition left behind by retreating troops, and at one point the young men were eager to follow and destroy an entire command who were apparently at their mercy, but their leader withheld them. They had now reached the buffalo country, and he always kept his main object in sight. He was extraordinarily calm. Doctor Grinnell was told by one of his men years afterward: "Little Wolf did not seem like a human being. He seemed like a bear." It is true that a man of his type in a crisis becomes spiritually transformed and moves as one in a dream.

At the Running Water the band divided, Dull Knife going toward Red Cloud agency. He was near Fort Robinson when he surrendered and met his sad fate. Little Wolf remained all winter in the Sand Hills, where there was plenty of game and no white men. Later he went to Montana and then to Pine Ridge, where he and his people remained in peace until they were removed to Lame Deer, Montana, and there he spent the remainder of his days. There is a clear sky beyond the clouds of racial prejudice, and in that final Court of Honor a noble soul like that of Little Wolf has a place.

Hole-in-the-Day[1]

IN the beginning of the nineteenth century, the Indian nations of the Northwest first experienced the pressure of civilization. At this period there were among them some brilliant leaders unknown to history, for the curious reason that they cordially received and welcomed the newcomers rather than opposed them. The only difficulties were those arising among the European nations themselves, and often involving the native tribes. Thus new environments brought new motives, and our temptations were increased manyfold with the new weapons, new goods, and above all the subtly destructive "spirit water."

Gradually it became known that the new race had a definite purpose, and that purpose was to chart and possess the whole country, regardless of the rights of its earlier inhabitants. Still the old chiefs cautioned their people to be patient, for, said they, the land is vast, both races can live on it, each in their own way. Let us therefore befriend them and trust to their friendship. While they reasoned thus, the temptations of graft and self-aggrandizement overtook some of the leaders.

Hole-in-the-Day (or Bug-o-nay-ki-shig) was born in the opening days of this era. The word "ki-shig" means either "day" or "sky", and the name is perhaps more correctly translated Hole-in-the-Sky. This gifted man inherited his name and much of his ability from his father, who was a war chief among the Ojibways,

---

[1] I wish to thank Reverend C. H. Beaulieu of Le Soeur, Minnesota, for much of the material used in this chapter.

a Napoleon of the common people, and who carried on a relentless warfare against the Sioux. And yet, as was our custom at the time, peaceful meetings were held every summer, at which representatives of the two tribes would recount to one another all the events that had come to pass during the preceding year.

Hole-in-the-Day the younger was a handsome man, tall and symmetrically formed, with much grace of manner and natural refinement. He was an astute student of diplomacy. The Ojibways allowed polygamy, and whether or not he approved the principle, he made political use of it by marrying the daughter of a chief in nearly every band. Through these alliances he held a controlling influence over the whole Ojibway nation. Reverend Claude H. Beaulieu says of him:

"Hole-in-the-Day was a man of distinguished appearance and native courtliness of manner. His voice was musical and magnetic, and with these qualities he had a subtle brain, a logical mind, and quite a remarkable gift of oratory. In speech he was not impassioned, but clear and convincing, and held fast the attention of his hearers."

It is of interest to note that his everyday name among his tribesmen was "The Boy." What a boy he must have been! I wonder if the name had the same significance as with the Sioux, who applied it to any man who performs a difficult duty with alertness, dash, and natural courage. "The Man" applies to one who adds to these qualities wisdom and maturity of judgment.

The Sioux tell many stories of both the elder and the younger Hole-in-the-Day. Once when The Boy was still under ten years of age, he was fishing on Gull Lake in a leaky birch-bark canoe. Presently there came such a burst of frantic war whoops that his father was startled. He could not think of anything but an attack by the dreaded Sioux. Seizing his weapons, he ran to the rescue of his son, only to find that the little fellow had caught a fish so large that it was pulling his canoe all over the lake. "Ugh," exclaimed the father, "if a mere fish scares you so badly, I fear you will never make a warrior!"

It is told of him that when he was very small, the father once brought home two bear cubs and gave them to him for pets. The Boy was feeding and getting acquainted with them outside his mother's birch-bark teepee, when suddenly he was heard to yell for help. The two little bears had treed The Boy and were waltzing around the tree. His mother scared them off, but again the father laughed at him for thinking that he could climb trees better than a bear.

The elder Hole-in-the-Day was a daring warrior and once attacked and scalped a Sioux who was carrying his pelts to the trading post, in full sight of his friends. Of course he was instantly pursued, and he leaped into a canoe which was lying near by and crossed to an island in the Mississippi River near Fort Snelling. When almost surrounded by Sioux warriors, he left the canoe and swam along the shore with only his nose above water, but as they were about to head him off he landed and hid behind the falling sheet of water known as Minnehaha Falls, thus saving his life.

It often happens that one who offers his life freely will after all die a natural death. The elder Hole-in-the-Day so died when The Boy was still a youth. Like Philip of Massachusetts, Chief Joseph the younger, and the brilliant Osceola, the mantle fell gracefully upon his shoulders, and he wore it during a short but eventful term of chieftainship. It was his to see the end of the original democracy on this continent. The clouds were fast thickening on the eastern horizon. The day of individualism and equity between man and man must yield to the terrific forces of civilization, the mass play of materialism, the cupidity of commerce with its twin brother politics. Under such conditions the younger Hole-in-the-Day undertook to guide his tribesmen. At first they were inclined to doubt the wisdom of so young a leader, but he soon proved a ready student of his people's traditions, and yet, like Spotted Tail and Little Crow, he adopted too willingly the white man's politics. He maintained the territory won from the Sioux by his predecessors. He negotiated treaties with the ability of a born diplomat, with one exception, and that exception cost him his life.

Like other able Indians who foresaw the inevitable downfall of their race, he favored a gradual change of customs leading to complete adoption of the white man's ways. In order to accustom the people to a new standard, he held that the chiefs must have authority and must be given compensation for their services. This was a serious departure from the old rule but was tacitly accepted, and in every treaty he made there was provision for himself in the way of a land grant or a cash payment. He early departed from the old idea of joint ownership with the Lake Superior Ojibways, because he foresaw that it would cause no end of trouble for the Mississippi River branch of which he was then the recognized head. But there were difficulties to come with the Leech Lake and Red Lake bands, who held aloof from his policy, and the question of boundaries began to arise.

In the first treaty negotiated with the government by young Hole-in-the-Day in 1855, a "surplus" was provided for the chiefs aside from the regular per capita payment, and this surplus was to be distributed in proportion to the number of Indians under each. Hole-in-the-Day had by far the largest enrollment, therefore he got the lion's share of this fund. Furthermore he received another sum set apart for the use of the "head chief", and these things did not look right to the tribe. In the very next treaty he provided himself with an annuity of one thousand dollars for twenty years, beside a section of land near the village of Crow Wing, and the government was induced to build him a good house upon this land. In his home he had many white servants and henchmen and really lived like a lord. He dressed well in native style with a touch of civilized elegance, wearing coat and leggings of fine broadcloth, linen shirt with collar, and, topping all, a handsome black or blue blanket. His moccasins were of the finest deerskin and beautifully worked. His long beautiful hair added much to his personal appearance. He was fond of entertaining and being entertained and was a favorite both among army officers and civilians. He was especially popular with the ladies, and this fact will appear later in the story.

At about this time, the United States government took it upon itself to put an end to warfare between the Sioux and Ojibways. A peace meeting was arranged at Fort Snelling, with the United States as mediator. When the representatives of the two nations met at this grand council, Hole-in-the-Day came as the head chief of his people, and with the other chiefs appeared in considerable pomp and dignity. The wives of the government officials were eager for admission to this unusual gathering, but when they arrived there was hardly any space left except next to the Sioux chiefs, and the white ladies soon crowded this space to overflowing. One of the Sioux remarked: "I thought this was to be a council of chiefs and braves, but I see many women among us." Thereupon the Ojibway arose and spoke in his courtliest manner. "The Ojibway chiefs will feel highly honored," said he, "if the ladies will consent to sit on our side."

Another sign of his alertness to gain favor among the whites was seen in the fact that he took part in the territorial campaigns, a most unusual thing for an Indian of that day. Being a man of means and influence, he was listened to with respect by the scattered white settlers in his vicinity. He would make a political speech through an interpreter, but would occasionally break loose in his broken English, and wind up with an invitation to drink in the following words: "Chentimen, you Pemicans (Republicans), come out and drink!"

From 1855 to 1864 Hole-in-the-Day was a well-known figure in Minnesota, and scarcely less so in Washington, for he visited the capital quite often on tribal affairs. As I have said before, he was an unusually handsome man, and was not unresponsive to flattery and the attentions of women. At the time of this incident he was perhaps thirty-five years old, but looked younger. He had called upon the President and was on his way back to his hotel, when he happened to pass the Treasury building just as the clerks were leaving for the day. He was immediately surrounded by an inquisitive throng. Among them was a handsome young woman who asked through the interpreter if the chief would consent to an interview about his people, to aid her in a paper she had promised to prepare.

Hole-in-the-Day replied: "If the beautiful lady is willing to risk calling on the chief at his hotel, her request will be granted." The lady went, and the result was so sudden and strong an attachment that both forgot all racial biases and differences of language and custom. She followed him as far as Minneapolis, and there the chief advised her to remain, for he feared the jealousy of some of his many wives. She died there, soon after giving birth to a son, who was brought up by a family named Woodbury; and some fifteen years ago I met the young man in Washington and was taken by him to call upon certain of his mother's relatives.

The ascendancy of Hole-in-the-Day was not gained entirely through the consent of his people, but largely by government favor, therefore there was strong suppressed resentment among his associate chiefs, and the Red Lake and Leech Lake bands, in fact, never acknowledged him as their head, while they suspected him of making treaties which involved some of their land. He was in personal danger from this source, and his life was twice attempted, but, though wounded, in each case he recovered. His popularity with Indian agents and officers lasted till the Republicans came into power in the sixties and there was a new deal. The chief no longer received the favors and tips to which he was accustomed; in fact he was in want of luxuries, and worse still, his pride was hurt by neglect. The new party had promised Christian treatment to the Indians, but it appeared that they were greater grafters than their predecessors, and unlike them kept everything for themselves, allowing no perquisites to any Indian chief.

In his indignation at this treatment, Hole-in-the-Day began exposing the frauds on his people, and so at a late day was converted to their defense. Perhaps he had not fully understood the nature of graft until he was in a position to view it from the outside. After all, he was excusable in seeking to maintain the dignity of his office, but he had departed from one of the fundamental rules of the race, namely: "Let no material gain be the motive or reward of public duty." He had wounded the ideals of his people beyond forgiveness, and he suffered the penalty; yet his courage was not diminished by the mistakes of his past. Like the Sioux chief Little Crow, he was called "the betrayer of his people", and like him he made a desperate effort to regain lost prestige, and turned savagely against the original betrayers of his confidence, the agents and Indian traders.

When the Sioux finally broke out in 1862, the first thought of the local politicians was to humiliate Hole-in-the-Day by arresting him and proclaiming some other "head chief" in his stead. In so doing they almost forced the Ojibways to fight under his leadership. The chief had no thought of alliance with the Sioux, and was wholly unaware of the proposed action of the military on pretense of such a conspiracy on his part. He was on his way to the agency in his own carriage when a runner warned him of his danger. He thereupon jumped down and instructed the driver to proceed. His coachman was arrested by a file of soldiers, who when they discovered their mistake went to his residence in search of him, but meanwhile he had sent runners in every direction to notify his warriors, and had moved his family across the Mississippi. When the military reached the river bank he was still in sight, and the lieutenant called upon him to surrender. When he refused, the soldiers were ordered to fire upon him, but he replied with his own rifle, and with a whoop disappeared among the pine groves.

It was remarkable how the whole tribe now rallied to the call of Hole-in-the-Day. He allowed no depredations to the young men under his leadership, but camped openly near the agency and awaited an explanation. Presently Judge Cooper of St. Paul, a personal friend of the chief, appeared, and later on the Assistant Secretary of the Interior, accompanied by Mr. Nicolay, private secretary of President Lincoln. Apparently that great humanitarian President saw the whole injustice of the proceeding against a loyal nation, and the difficulty was at an end.

Through the treaties of 1864, 1867, and 1868 was accomplished the final destiny of the Mississippi River Ojibways. Hole-in-the-Day was against their removal to what is now White Earth reservation, but he was defeated in this and realized that the new turn of events meant the downfall of his race. He declared that he would never go on the new reservation, and he kept his word. He remained on one of his land grants near Crow Wing. As the other chiefs assumed more power, the old feeling of suspicion and hatred became stronger, especially among the Pillager and Red Lake bands. One day he was waylaid and shot by a party of these disaffected Indians. He uttered a whoop and fell dead from his buggy.

Thus died one of the most brilliant chiefs of the Northwest, who never defended his birthright by force of arms, although almost compelled to do so. He succeeded in diplomacy so long as he was the recognized head of his people. Since we have not passed over his weaknesses, he should be given credit for much insight in causing the article prohibiting the introduction of liquor into the Indian country to be inserted into the treaty of 1858. I think it was in 1910 that this forgotten provision was discovered and again enforced over a large expanse of territory occupied by whites, it being found that the provision had never been repealed.

Although he left many children, none seem to have made their mark, yet it may be that in one of his descendants that undaunted spirit will rise again.

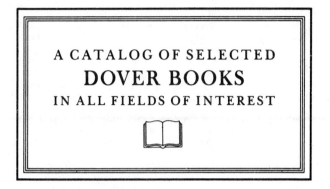

A CATALOG OF SELECTED
DOVER BOOKS
IN ALL FIELDS OF INTEREST

A CATALOG OF SELECTED DOVER
BOOKS IN ALL FIELDS OF INTEREST

CONCERNING THE SPIRITUAL IN ART, Wassily Kandinsky. Pioneering work by father of abstract art. Thoughts on color theory, nature of art. Analysis of earlier masters. 12 illustrations. 80pp. of text. 5⅜ × 8½. 23411-8 Pa. $3.95

ANIMALS: 1,419 Copyright-Free Illustrations of Mammals, Birds, Fish, Insects, etc., Jim Harter (ed.). Clear wood engravings present, in extremely lifelike poses, over 1,000 species of animals. One of the most extensive pictorial sourcebooks of its kind. Captions. Index. 284pp. 9 × 12. 23766-4 Pa. $12.95

CELTIC ART: The Methods of Construction, George Bain. Simple geometric techniques for making Celtic interlacements, spirals, Kells-type initials, animals, humans, etc. Over 500 illustrations. 160pp. 9 × 12. (USO) 22923-8 Pa. $9.95

AN ATLAS OF ANATOMY FOR ARTISTS, Fritz Schider. Most thorough reference work on art anatomy in the world. Hundreds of illustrations, including selections from works by Vesalius, Leonardo, Goya, Ingres, Michelangelo, others. 593 illustrations. 192pp. 7⅛ × 10¼. 20241-0 Pa. $9.95

CELTIC HAND STROKE-BY-STROKE (Irish Half-Uncial from "The Book of Kells"): An Arthur Baker Calligraphy Manual, Arthur Baker. Complete guide to creating each letter of the alphabet in distinctive Celtic manner. Covers hand position, strokes, pens, inks, paper, more. Illustrated. 48pp. 8¼ × 11. 24336-2 Pa. $3.95

EASY ORIGAMI, John Montroll. Charming collection of 32 projects (hat, cup, pelican, piano, swan, many more) specially designed for the novice origami hobbyist. Clearly illustrated easy-to-follow instructions insure that even beginning papercrafters will achieve successful results. 48pp. 8¼ × 11. 27298-2 Pa. $2.95

THE COMPLETE BOOK OF BIRDHOUSE CONSTRUCTION FOR WOOD-WORKERS, Scott D. Campbell. Detailed instructions, illustrations, tables. Also data on bird habitat and instinct patterns. Bibliography. 3 tables. 63 illustrations in 15 figures. 48pp. 5¼ × 8½. 24407-5 Pa. $1.95

BLOOMINGDALE'S ILLUSTRATED 1886 CATALOG: Fashions, Dry Goods and Housewares, Bloomingdale Brothers. Famed merchants' extremely rare catalog depicting about 1,700 products: clothing, housewares, firearms, dry goods, jewelry, more. Invaluable for dating, identifying vintage items. Also, copyright-free graphics for artists, designers. Co-published with Henry Ford Museum & Greenfield Village. 160pp. 8¼ × 11. 25780-0 Pa. $9.95

HISTORIC COSTUME IN PICTURES, Braun & Schneider. Over 1,450 costumed figures in clearly detailed engravings—from dawn of civilization to end of 19th century. Captions. Many folk costumes. 256pp. 8⅜ × 11¾. 23150-X Pa. $11.95

STICKLEY CRAFTSMAN FURNITURE CATALOGS, Gustav Stickley and L. & J. G. Stickley. Beautiful, functional furniture in two authentic catalogs from 1910. 594 illustrations, including 277 photos, show settles, rockers, armchairs, reclining chairs, bookcases, desks, tables. 183pp. 6½ × 9¼. 23838-5 Pa. $9.95

AMERICAN LOCOMOTIVES IN HISTORIC PHOTOGRAPHS: 1858 to 1949, Ron Ziel (ed.). A rare collection of 126 meticulously detailed official photographs, called "builder portraits," of American locomotives that majestically chronicle the rise of steam locomotive power in America. Introduction. Detailed captions. xi + 129pp. 9 × 12. 27393-8 Pa. $12.95

AMERICA'S LIGHTHOUSES: An Illustrated History, Francis Ross Holland, Jr. Delightfully written, profusely illustrated fact-filled survey of over 200 American lighthouses since 1716. History, anecdotes, technological advances, more. 240pp. 8 × 10¾. 25576-X Pa. $11.95

TOWARDS A NEW ARCHITECTURE, Le Corbusier. Pioneering manifesto by founder of "International School." Technical and aesthetic theories, views of industry, economics, relation of form to function, "mass-production split" and much more. Profusely illustrated. 320pp. 6⅛ × 9¼. (USO) 25023-7 Pa. $9.95

HOW THE OTHER HALF LIVES, Jacob Riis. Famous journalistic record, exposing poverty and degradation of New York slums around 1900, by major social reformer. 100 striking and influential photographs. 233pp. 10 × 7⅞. 22012-5 Pa $10.95

FRUIT KEY AND TWIG KEY TO TREES AND SHRUBS, William M. Harlow. One of the handiest and most widely used identification aids. Fruit key covers 120 deciduous and evergreen species; twig key 160 deciduous species. Easily used. Over 300 photographs. 126pp. 5⅜ × 8½. 20511-8 Pa. $3.95

COMMON BIRD SONGS, Dr. Donald J. Borror. Songs of 60 most common U.S. birds: robins, sparrows, cardinals, bluejays, finches, more—arranged in order of increasing complexity. Up to 9 variations of songs of each species. Cassette and manual 99911-4 $8.95

ORCHIDS AS HOUSE PLANTS, Rebecca Tyson Northen. Grow cattleyas and many other kinds of orchids—in a window, in a case, or under artificial light. 63 illustrations. 148pp. 5⅜ × 8½. 23261-1 Pa. $4.95

MONSTER MAZES, Dave Phillips. Masterful mazes at four levels of difficulty. Avoid deadly perils and evil creatures to find magical treasures. Solutions for all 32 exciting illustrated puzzles. 48pp. 8¼ × 11. 26005-4 Pa. $2.95

MOZART'S DON GIOVANNI (DOVER OPERA LIBRETTO SERIES), Wolfgang Amadeus Mozart. Introduced and translated by Ellen H. Bleiler. Standard Italian libretto, with complete English translation. Convenient and thoroughly portable—an ideal companion for reading along with a recording or the performance itself. Introduction. List of characters. Plot summary. 121pp. 5¼ × 8½. 24944-1 Pa. $2.95

TECHNICAL MANUAL AND DICTIONARY OF CLASSICAL BALLET, Gail Grant. Defines, explains, comments on steps, movements, poses and concepts. 15-page pictorial section. Basic book for student, viewer. 127pp. 5⅜ × 8½. 21843-0 Pa. $4.95

BRASS INSTRUMENTS: Their History and Development, Anthony Baines. Authoritative, updated survey of the evolution of trumpets, trombones, bugles, cornets, French horns, tubas and other brass wind instruments. Over 140 illustrations and 48 music examples. Corrected and updated by author. New preface. Bibliography. 320pp. 5⅜ × 8½. 27574-4 Pa. $9.95

HOLLYWOOD GLAMOR PORTRAITS, John Kobal (ed.). 145 photos from 1926–49. Harlow, Gable, Bogart, Bacall; 94 stars in all. Full background on photographers, technical aspects. 160pp. 8⅞ × 11¼. 23352-9 Pa. $11.95

MAX AND MORITZ, Wilhelm Busch. Great humor classic in both German and English. Also 10 other works: "Cat and Mouse," "Plisch and Plumm," etc. 216pp. 5⅜ × 8½. 20181-3 Pa. $5.95

THE RAVEN AND OTHER FAVORITE POEMS, Edgar Allan Poe. Over 40 of the author's most memorable poems: "The Bells," "Ulalume," "Israfel," "To Helen," "The Conqueror Worm," "Eldorado," "Annabel Lee," many more. Alphabetic lists of titles and first lines. 64pp. 5³⁄₁₆ × 8¼. 26685-0 Pa. $1.00

SEVEN SCIENCE FICTION NOVELS, H. G. Wells. The standard collection of the great novels. Complete, unabridged. First Men in the Moon, Island of Dr. Moreau, War of the Worlds, Food of the Gods, Invisible Man, Time Machine, In the Days of the Comet. Total of 1,015pp. 5⅜ × 8½. (USO) 20264-X Clothbd. $29.95

AMULETS AND SUPERSTITIONS, E. A. Wallis Budge. Comprehensive discourse on origin, powers of amulets in many ancient cultures: Arab, Persian, Babylonian, Assyrian, Egyptian, Gnostic, Hebrew, Phoenician, Syriac, etc. Covers cross, swastika, crucifix, seals, rings, stones, etc. 584pp. 5⅜ × 8½. 23573-4 Pa. $12.95

RUSSIAN STORIES/PYCCKNE PACCKA3bl: A Dual-Language Book, edited by Gleb Struve. Twelve tales by such masters as Chekhov, Tolstoy, Dostoevsky, Pushkin, others. Excellent word-for-word English translations on facing pages, plus teaching and study aids, Russian/English vocabulary, biographical/critical introductions, more. 416pp. 5⅜ × 8½. 26244-8 Pa. $8.95

PHILADELPHIA THEN AND NOW: 60 Sites Photographed in the Past and Present, Kenneth Finkel and Susan Oyama. Rare photographs of City Hall, Logan Square, Independence Hall, Betsy Ross House, other landmarks juxtaposed with contemporary views. Captures changing face of historic city. Introduction. Captions. 128pp. 8¼ × 11. 25790-8 Pa. $9.95

AIA ARCHITECTURAL GUIDE TO NASSAU AND SUFFOLK COUNTIES, LONG ISLAND, The American Institute of Architects, Long Island Chapter, and the Society for the Preservation of Long Island Antiquities. Comprehensive, well-researched and generously illustrated volume brings to life over three centuries of Long Island's great architectural heritage. More than 240 photographs with authoritative, extensively detailed captions. 176pp. 8¼ × 11. 26946-9 Pa. $14.95

NORTH AMERICAN INDIAN LIFE: Customs and Traditions of 23 Tribes, Elsie Clews Parsons (ed.). 27 fictionalized essays by noted anthropologists examine religion, customs, government, additional facets of life among the Winnebago, Crow, Zuni, Eskimo, other tribes. 480pp. 6⅛ × 9¼. 27377-6 Pa. $10.95

FRANK LLOYD WRIGHT'S HOLLYHOCK HOUSE, Donald Hoffmann. Lavishly illustrated, carefully documented study of one of Wright's most controversial residential designs. Over 120 photographs, floor plans, elevations, etc. Detailed perceptive text by noted Wright scholar. Index. 128pp. 9¼ × 10¾.
27133-1 Pa. $11.95

THE MALE AND FEMALE FIGURE IN MOTION: 60 Classic Photographic Sequences, Eadweard Muybridge. 60 true-action photographs of men and women walking, running, climbing, bending, turning, etc., reproduced from rare 19th-century masterpiece. vi + 121pp. 9 × 12.
24745-7 Pa. $10.95

1001 QUESTIONS ANSWERED ABOUT THE SEASHORE, N. J. Berrill and Jacquelyn Berrill. Queries answered about dolphins, sea snails, sponges, starfish, fishes, shore birds, many others. Covers appearance, breeding, growth, feeding, much more. 305pp. 5¼ × 8¼.
23366-9 Pa. $7.95

GUIDE TO OWL WATCHING IN NORTH AMERICA, Donald S. Heintzelman. Superb guide offers complete data and descriptions of 19 species: barn owl, screech owl, snowy owl, many more. Expert coverage of owl-watching equipment, conservation, migrations and invasions, etc. Guide to observing sites. 84 illustrations. xiii + 193pp. 5⅜ × 8½.
27344-X Pa. $8.95

MEDICINAL AND OTHER USES OF NORTH AMERICAN PLANTS: A Historical Survey with Special Reference to the Eastern Indian Tribes, Charlotte Erichsen-Brown. Chronological historical citations document 500 years of usage of plants, trees, shrubs native to eastern Canada, northeastern U.S. Also complete identifying information. 343 illustrations. 544pp. 6½ × 9¼.
25951-X Pa. $12.95

STORYBOOK MAZES, Dave Phillips. 23 stories and mazes on two-page spreads: Wizard of Oz, Treasure Island, Robin Hood, etc. Solutions. 64pp. 8¼ × 11.
23628-5 Pa. $2.95

NEGRO FOLK MUSIC, U.S.A., Harold Courlander. Noted folklorist's scholarly yet readable analysis of rich and varied musical tradition. Includes authentic versions of over 40 folk songs. Valuable bibliography and discography. xi + 324pp. 5⅜ × 8½.
27350-4 Pa. $7.95

MOVIE-STAR PORTRAITS OF THE FORTIES, John Kobal (ed.). 163 glamor, studio photos of 106 stars of the 1940s: Rita Hayworth, Ava Gardner, Marlon Brando, Clark Gable, many more. 176pp. 8⅜ × 11¼.
23546-7 Pa. $11.95

BENCHLEY LOST AND FOUND, Robert Benchley. Finest humor from early 30s, about pet peeves, child psychologists, post office and others. Mostly unavailable elsewhere. 73 illustrations by Peter Arno and others. 183pp. 5⅜ × 8½.
22410-4 Pa. $5.95

YEKL and THE IMPORTED BRIDEGROOM AND OTHER STORIES OF YIDDISH NEW YORK, Abraham Cahan. Film Hester Street based on Yekl (1896). Novel, other stories among first about Jewish immigrants on N.Y.'s East Side. 240pp. 5⅜ × 8½.
22427-9 Pa. $6.95

SELECTED POEMS, Walt Whitman. Generous sampling from *Leaves of Grass*. Twenty-four poems include "I Hear America Singing," "Song of the Open Road," "I Sing the Body Electric," "When Lilacs Last in the Dooryard Bloom'd," "O Captain! My Captain!"—all reprinted from an authoritative edition. Lists of titles and first lines. 128pp. 5³⁄₁₆ × 8¼.
26878-0 Pa. $1.00

THE BEST TALES OF HOFFMANN, E. T. A. Hoffmann. 10 of Hoffmann's most important stories: "Nutcracker and the King of Mice," "The Golden Flowerpot," etc. 458pp. 5⅜ × 8½. 21793-0 Pa. $8.95

FROM FETISH TO GOD IN ANCIENT EGYPT, E. A. Wallis Budge. Rich detailed survey of Egyptian conception of "God" and gods, magic, cult of animals, Osiris, more. Also, superb English translations of hymns and legends. 240 illustrations. 545pp. 5⅜ × 8½. 25803-3 Pa. $11.95

FRENCH STORIES/CONTES FRANÇAIS: A Dual-Language Book, Wallace Fowlie. Ten stories by French masters, Voltaire to Camus: "Micromegas" by Voltaire; "The Atheist's Mass" by Balzac; "Minuet" by de Maupassant; "The Guest" by Camus, six more. Excellent English translations on facing pages. Also French-English vocabulary list, exercises, more. 352pp. 5⅜ × 8½. 26443-2 Pa. $8.95

CHICAGO AT THE TURN OF THE CENTURY IN PHOTOGRAPHS: 122 Historic Views from the Collections of the Chicago Historical Society, Larry A. Viskochil. Rare large-format prints offer detailed views of City Hall, State Street, the Loop, Hull House, Union Station, many other landmarks, circa 1904–1913. Introduction. Captions. Maps. 144pp. 9⅜ × 12¼. 24656-6 Pa. $12.95

OLD BROOKLYN IN EARLY PHOTOGRAPHS, 1865–1929, William Lee Younger. Luna Park, Gravesend race track, construction of Grand Army Plaza, moving of Hotel Brighton, etc. 157 previously unpublished photographs. 165pp. 8⅜ × 11¼. 23587-4 Pa. $13.95

THE MYTHS OF THE NORTH AMERICAN INDIANS, Lewis Spence. Rich anthology of the myths and legends of the Algonquins, Iroquois, Pawnees and Sioux, prefaced by an extensive historical and ethnological commentary. 36 illustrations. 480pp. 5⅜ × 8½. 25967-6 Pa. $8.95

AN ENCYCLOPEDIA OF BATTLES: Accounts of Over 1,560 Battles from 1479 B.C. to the Present, David Eggenberger. Essential details of every major battle in recorded history from the first battle of Megiddo in 1479 B.C. to Grenada in 1984. List of Battle Maps. New Appendix covering the years 1967–1984. Index. 99 illustrations. 544pp. 6½ × 9¼. 24913-1 Pa. $14.95

SAILING ALONE AROUND THE WORLD, Captain Joshua Slocum. First man to sail around the world, alone, in small boat. One of great feats of seamanship told in delightful manner. 67 illustrations. 294pp. 5⅜ × 8½. 20326-3 Pa. $5.95

ANARCHISM AND OTHER ESSAYS, Emma Goldman. Powerful, penetrating, prophetic essays on direct action, role of minorities, prison reform, puritan hypocrisy, violence, etc. 271pp. 5⅜ × 8½. 22484-8 Pa. $5.95

MYTHS OF THE HINDUS AND BUDDHISTS, Ananda K. Coomaraswamy and Sister Nivedita. Great stories of the epics; deeds of Krishna, Shiva, taken from puranas, Vedas, folk tales; etc. 32 illustrations. 400pp. 5⅜ × 8½. 21759-0 Pa. $9.95

BEYOND PSYCHOLOGY, Otto Rank. Fear of death, desire of immortality, nature of sexuality, social organization, creativity, according to Rankian system. 291pp. 5⅜ × 8½. 20485-5 Pa. $8.95

A THEOLOGICO-POLITICAL TREATISE, Benedict Spinoza. Also contains unfinished Political Treatise. Great classic on religious liberty, theory of government on common consent. R. Elwes translation. Total of 421pp. 5⅜ × 8½. 20249-6 Pa. $8.95

MY BONDAGE AND MY FREEDOM, Frederick Douglass. Born a slave, Douglass became outspoken force in antislavery movement. The best of Douglass' autobiographies. Graphic description of slave life. 464pp. 5⅜ × 8½. 22457-0 Pa. **$8.95**

FOLLOWING THE EQUATOR: A Journey Around the World, Mark Twain. Fascinating humorous account of 1897 voyage to Hawaii, Australia, India, New Zealand, etc. Ironic, bemused reports on peoples, customs, climate, flora and fauna, politics, much more. 197 illustrations. 720pp. 5⅜ × 8½. 26113-1 Pa. **$15.95**

THE PEOPLE CALLED SHAKERS, Edward D. Andrews. Definitive study of Shakers: origins, beliefs, practices, dances, social organization, furniture and crafts, etc. 33 illustrations. 351pp. 5⅜ × 8½. 21081-2 Pa. **$8.95**

THE MYTHS OF GREECE AND ROME, H. A. Guerber. A classic of mythology, generously illustrated, long prized for its simple, graphic, accurate retelling of the principal myths of Greece and Rome, and for its commentary on their origins and significance. With 64 illustrations by Michelangelo, Raphael, Titian, Rubens, Canova, Bernini and others. 480pp. 5⅜ × 8½. 27584-1 Pa. **$9.95**

PSYCHOLOGY OF MUSIC, Carl E. Seashore. Classic work discusses music as a medium from psychological viewpoint. Clear treatment of physical acoustics, auditory apparatus, sound perception, development of musical skills, nature of musical feeling, host of other topics. 88 figures. 408pp. 5⅜ × 8½. 21851-1 Pa. **$9.95**

THE PHILOSOPHY OF HISTORY, Georg W. Hegel. Great classic of Western thought develops concept that history is not chance but rational process, the evolution of freedom. 457pp. 5⅜ × 8½. 20112-0 Pa. **$9.95**

THE BOOK OF TEA, Kakuzo Okakura. Minor classic of the Orient: entertaining, charming explanation, interpretation of traditional Japanese culture in terms of tea ceremony. 94pp. 5⅜ × 8½. 20070-1 Pa. **$3.95**

LIFE IN ANCIENT EGYPT, Adolf Erman. Fullest, most thorough, detailed older account with much not in more recent books, domestic life, religion, magic, medicine, commerce, much more. Many illustrations reproduce tomb paintings, carvings, hieroglyphs, etc. 597pp. 5⅜ × 8½. 22632-8 Pa. **$10.95**

SUNDIALS, Their Theory and Construction, Albert Waugh. Far and away the best, most thorough coverage of ideas, mathematics concerned, types, construction, adjusting anywhere. Simple, nontechnical treatment allows even children to build several of these dials. Over 100 illustrations. 230pp. 5⅜ × 8½. 22947-5 Pa. **$7.95**

DYNAMICS OF FLUIDS IN POROUS MEDIA, Jacob Bear. For advanced students of ground water hydrology, soil mechanics and physics, drainage and irrigation engineering, and more. 335 illustrations. Exercises, with answers. 784pp. 6⅛ × 9¼. 65675-6 Pa. **$19.95**

SONGS OF EXPERIENCE: Facsimile Reproduction with 26 Plates in Full Color, William Blake. 26 full-color plates from a rare 1826 edition. Includes "The Tyger," "London," "Holy Thursday," and other poems. Printed text of poems. 48pp. 5¼ × 7. 24636-1 Pa. **$4.95**

OLD-TIME VIGNETTES IN FULL COLOR, Carol Belanger Grafton (ed.). Over 390 charming, often sentimental illustrations, selected from archives of Victorian graphics—pretty women posing, children playing, food, flowers, kittens and puppies, smiling cherubs, birds and butterflies, much more. All copyright-free. 48pp. 9¼ × 12¼. 27269-9 Pa. **$5.95**

PERSPECTIVE FOR ARTISTS, Rex Vicat Cole. Depth, perspective of sky and sea, shadows, much more, not usually covered. 391 diagrams, 81 reproductions of drawings and paintings. 279pp. 5⅜ × 8½. 22487-2 Pa. $6.95

DRAWING THE LIVING FIGURE, Joseph Sheppard. Innovative approach to artistic anatomy focuses on specifics of surface anatomy, rather than muscles and bones. Over 170 drawings of live models in front, back and side views, and in widely varying poses. Accompanying diagrams. 177 illustrations. Introduction. Index. 144pp. 8⅜ × 11¼. 26723-7 Pa. $8.95

GOTHIC AND OLD ENGLISH ALPHABETS: 100 Complete Fonts, Dan X. Solo. Add power, elegance to posters, signs, other graphics with 100 stunning copyright-free alphabets: Blackstone, Dolbey, Germania, 97 more—including many lower-case, numerals, punctuation marks. 104pp. 8⅜ × 11. 24695-7 Pa. $8.95

HOW TO DO BEADWORK, Mary White. Fundamental book on craft from simple projects to five-bead chains and woven works. 106 illustrations. 142pp. 5⅜ × 8. 20697-1 Pa. $4.95

THE BOOK OF WOOD CARVING, Charles Marshall Sayers. Finest book for beginners discusses fundamentals and offers 34 designs. "Absolutely first rate . . . well thought out and well executed."—E. J. Tangerman. 118pp. 7¾ × 10⅝. 23654-4 Pa. $5.95

ILLUSTRATED CATALOG OF CIVIL WAR MILITARY GOODS: Union Army Weapons, Insignia, Uniform Accessories, and Other Equipment, Schuyler, Hartley, and Graham. Rare, profusely illustrated 1846 catalog includes Union Army uniform and dress regulations, arms and ammunition, coats, insignia, flags, swords, rifles, etc. 226 illustrations. 160pp. 9 × 12. 24939-5 Pa. $10.95

WOMEN'S FASHIONS OF THE EARLY 1900s: An Unabridged Republication of "New York Fashions, 1909," National Cloak & Suit Co. Rare catalog of mail-order fashions documents women's and children's clothing styles shortly after the turn of the century. Captions offer full descriptions, prices. Invaluable resource for fashion, costume historians. Approximately 725 illustrations. 128pp. 8⅜ × 11¼. 27276-1 Pa. $11.95

THE 1912 AND 1915 GUSTAV STICKLEY FURNITURE CATALOGS, Gustav Stickley. With over 200 detailed illustrations and descriptions, these two catalogs are essential reading and reference materials and identification guides for Stickley furniture. Captions cite materials, dimensions and prices. 112pp. 6½ × 9¼. 26676-1 Pa. $9.95

EARLY AMERICAN LOCOMOTIVES, John H. White, Jr. Finest locomotive engravings from early 19th century: historical (1804–74), main-line (after 1870), special, foreign, etc. 147 plates. 142pp. 11⅜ × 8¼. 22772-3 Pa. $10.95

THE TALL SHIPS OF TODAY IN PHOTOGRAPHS, Frank O. Braynard. Lavishly illustrated tribute to nearly 100 majestic contemporary sailing vessels: Amerigo Vespucci, Clearwater, Constitution, Eagle, Mayflower, Sea Cloud, Victory, many more. Authoritative captions provide statistics, background on each ship. 190 black-and-white photographs and illustrations. Introduction. 128pp. 8⅜ × 11¼. 27163-3 Pa. $13.95

EARLY NINETEENTH-CENTURY CRAFTS AND TRADES, Peter Stockham (ed.). Extremely rare 1807 volume describes to youngsters the crafts and trades of the day: brickmaker, weaver, dressmaker, bookbinder, ropemaker, saddler, many more. Quaint prose, charming illustrations for each craft. 20 black-and-white line illustrations. 192pp. 4⅝ × 6. 27293-1 Pa. $4.95

VICTORIAN FASHIONS AND COSTUMES FROM HARPER'S BAZAR, 1867–1898, Stella Blum (ed.). Day costumes, evening wear, sports clothes, shoes, hats, other accessories in over 1,000 detailed engravings. 320pp. 9⅜ × 12¼. 22990-4 Pa. $13.95

GUSTAV STICKLEY, THE CRAFTSMAN, Mary Ann Smith. Superb study surveys broad scope of Stickley's achievement, especially in architecture. Design philosophy, rise and fall of the Craftsman empire, descriptions and floor plans for many Craftsman houses, more. 86 black-and-white halftones. 31 line illustrations. Introduction. 208pp. 6½ × 9¼. 27210-9 Pa. $9.95

THE LONG ISLAND RAIL ROAD IN EARLY PHOTOGRAPHS, Ron Ziel. Over 220 rare photos, informative text document origin (1844) and development of rail service on Long Island. Vintage views of early trains, locomotives, stations, passengers, crews, much more. Captions. 8⅞ × 11¾. 26301-0 Pa. $13.95

THE BOOK OF OLD SHIPS: From Egyptian Galleys to Clipper Ships, Henry B. Culver. Superb, authoritative history of sailing vessels, with 80 magnificent line illustrations. Galley, bark, caravel, longship, whaler, many more. Detailed, informative text on each vessel by noted naval historian. Introduction. 256pp. 5⅜ × 8½. 27332-6 Pa. $6.95

TEN BOOKS ON ARCHITECTURE, Vitruvius. The most important book ever written on architecture. Early Roman aesthetics, technology, classical orders, site selection, all other aspects. Morgan translation. 331pp. 5⅜ × 8½. 20645-9 Pa. $8.95

THE HUMAN FIGURE IN MOTION, Eadweard Muybridge. More than 4,500 stopped-action photos, in action series, showing undraped men, women, children jumping, lying down, throwing, sitting, wrestling, carrying, etc. 390pp. 7⅞ × 10⅝. 20204-6 Clothbd. $24.95

TREES OF THE EASTERN AND CENTRAL UNITED STATES AND CANADA, William M. Harlow. Best one-volume guide to 140 trees. Full descriptions, woodlore, range, etc. Over 600 illustrations. Handy size. 288pp. 4½ × 6⅜. 20395-6 Pa. $5.95

SONGS OF WESTERN BIRDS, Dr. Donald J. Borror. Complete song and call repertoire of 60 western species, including flycatchers, juncoes, cactus wrens, many more—includes fully illustrated booklet. Cassette and manual 99913-0 $8.95

GROWING AND USING HERBS AND SPICES, Milo Miloradovich. Versatile handbook provides all the information needed for cultivation and use of all the herbs and spices available in North America. 4 illustrations. Index. Glossary. 236pp. 5⅜ × 8½. 25058-X Pa. $6.95

BIG BOOK OF MAZES AND LABYRINTHS, Walter Shepherd. 50 mazes and labyrinths in all—classical, solid, ripple, and more—in one great volume. Perfect inexpensive puzzler for clever youngsters. Full solutions. 112pp. 8⅛ × 11. 22951-3 Pa. $4.95

PIANO TUNING, J. Cree Fischer. Clearest, best book for beginner, amateur. Simple repairs, raising dropped notes, tuning by easy method of flattened fifths. No previous skills needed. 4 illustrations. 201pp. 5⅜ × 8½.   23267-0 Pa. $5.95

A SOURCE BOOK IN THEATRICAL HISTORY, A. M. Nagler. Contemporary observers on acting, directing, make-up, costuming, stage props, machinery, scene design, from Ancient Greece to Chekhov. 611pp. 5⅜ × 8½.   20515-0 Pa. $11.95

THE COMPLETE NONSENSE OF EDWARD LEAR, Edward Lear. All nonsense limericks, zany alphabets, Owl and Pussycat, songs, nonsense botany, etc., illustrated by Lear. Total of 320pp. 5⅜ × 8½. (USO)   20167-8 Pa. $6.95

VICTORIAN PARLOUR POETRY: An Annotated Anthology, Michael R. Turner. 117 gems by Longfellow, Tennyson, Browning, many lesser-known poets. "The Village Blacksmith," "Curfew Must Not Ring Tonight," "Only a Baby Small," dozens more, often difficult to find elsewhere. Index of poets, titles, first lines. xxiii + 325pp. 5⅜ × 8¼.   27044-0 Pa. $8.95

DUBLINERS, James Joyce. Fifteen stories offer vivid, tightly focused observations of the lives of Dublin's poorer classes. At least one, "The Dead," is considered a masterpiece. Reprinted complete and unabridged from standard edition. 160pp. 5³⁄₁₆ × 8¼.   26870-5 Pa. $1.00

THE HAUNTED MONASTERY and THE CHINESE MAZE MURDERS, Robert van Gulik. Two full novels by van Gulik, set in 7th-century China, continue adventures of Judge Dee and his companions. An evil Taoist monastery, seemingly supernatural events; overgrown topiary maze hides strange crimes. 27 illustrations. 328pp. 5⅜ × 8½.   23502-5 Pa. $7.95

THE BOOK OF THE SACRED MAGIC OF ABRAMELIN THE MAGE, translated by S. MacGregor Mathers. Medieval manuscript of ceremonial magic. Basic document in Aleister Crowley, Golden Dawn groups. 268pp. 5⅜ × 8½.   23211-5 Pa. $8.95

NEW RUSSIAN-ENGLISH AND ENGLISH-RUSSIAN DICTIONARY, M. A. O'Brien. This is a remarkably handy Russian dictionary, containing a surprising amount of information, including over 70,000 entries. 366pp. 4½ × 6⅛.   20208-9 Pa. $9.95

HISTORIC HOMES OF THE AMERICAN PRESIDENTS, Second, Revised Edition, Irvin Haas. A traveler's guide to American Presidential homes, most open to the public, depicting and describing homes occupied by every American President from George Washington to George Bush. With visiting hours, admission charges, travel routes. 175 photographs. Index. 160pp. 8¼ × 11. 26751-2 Pa. $10.95

NEW YORK IN THE FORTIES, Andreas Feininger. 162 brilliant photographs by the well-known photographer, formerly with *Life* magazine. Commuters, shoppers, Times Square at night, much else from city at its peak. Captions by John von Hartz. 181pp. 9¼ × 10¾.   23585-8 Pa. $12.95

INDIAN SIGN LANGUAGE, William Tomkins. Over 525 signs developed by Sioux and other tribes. Written instructions and diagrams. Also 290 pictographs. 111pp. 6⅛ × 9¼.   22029-X Pa. $3.50

CATALOG OF DOVER BOOKS

ANATOMY: A Complete Guide for Artists, Joseph Sheppard. A master of figure drawing shows artists how to render human anatomy convincingly. Over 460 illustrations. 224pp. 8⅜ × 11¼. 27279-6 Pa. $10.95

MEDIEVAL CALLIGRAPHY: Its History and Technique, Marc Drogin. Spirited history, comprehensive instruction manual covers 13 styles (ca. 4th century thru 15th). Excellent photographs; directions for duplicating medieval techniques with modern tools. 224pp. 8⅜ × 11¼. 26142-5 Pa. $11.95

DRIED FLOWERS: How to Prepare Them, Sarah Whitlock and Martha Rankin. Complete instructions on how to use silica gel, meal and borax, perlite aggregate, sand and borax, glycerine and water to create attractive permanent flower arrangements. 12 illustrations. 32pp. 5⅜ × 8½. 21802-3 Pa. $1.00

EASY-TO-MAKE BIRD FEEDERS FOR WOODWORKERS, Scott D. Campbell. Detailed, simple-to-use guide for designing, constructing, caring for and using feeders. Text, illustrations for 12 classic and contemporary designs. 96pp. 5⅜ × 8½. 25847-5 Pa. $2.95

OLD-TIME CRAFTS AND TRADES, Peter Stockham. An 1807 book created to teach children about crafts and trades open to them as future careers. It describes in detailed, nontechnical terms 24 different occupations, among them coachmaker, gardener, hairdresser, lacemaker, shoemaker, wheelwright, copper-plate printer, milliner, trunkmaker, merchant and brewer. Finely detailed engravings illustrate each occupation. 192pp. 4⅝ × 6. 27398-9 Pa. $4.95

THE HISTORY OF UNDERCLOTHES, C. Willett Cunnington and Phyllis Cunnington. Fascinating, well-documented survey covering six centuries of English undergarments, enhanced with over 100 illustrations: 12th-century laced-up bodice, footed long drawers (1795), 19th-century bustles, 19th-century corsets for men, Victorian "bust improvers," much more. 272pp. 5⅜ × 8¼. 27124-2 Pa. $9.95

ARTS AND CRAFTS FURNITURE: The Complete Brooks Catalog of 1912, Brooks Manufacturing Co. Photos and detailed descriptions of more than 150 now very collectible furniture designs from the Arts and Crafts movement depict davenports, settees, buffets, desks, tables, chairs, bedsteads, dressers and more, all built of solid, quarter-sawed oak. Invaluable for students and enthusiasts of antiques, Americana and the decorative arts. 80pp. 6½ × 9¼. 27471-3 Pa. $7.95

HOW WE INVENTED THE AIRPLANE: An Illustrated History, Orville Wright. Fascinating firsthand account covers early experiments, construction of planes and motors, first flights, much more. Introduction and commentary by Fred C. Kelly. 76 photographs. 96pp. 8¼ × 11. 25662-6 Pa. $8.95

THE ARTS OF THE SAILOR: Knotting, Splicing and Ropework, Hervey Garrett Smith. Indispensable shipboard reference covers tools, basic knots and useful hitches; handsewing and canvas work, more. Over 100 illustrations. Delightful reading for sea lovers. 256pp. 5⅜ × 8½. 26440-8 Pa. $7.95

FRANK LLOYD WRIGHT'S FALLINGWATER: The House and Its History, Second, Revised Edition, Donald Hoffmann. A total revision—both in text and illustrations—of the standard document on Fallingwater, the boldest, most personal architectural statement of Wright's mature years, updated with valuable new material from the recently opened Frank Lloyd Wright Archives. "Fascinating"—*The New York Times.* 116 illustrations. 128pp. 9¼ × 10¾. 27430-6 Pa. $10.95

PHOTOGRAPHIC SKETCHBOOK OF THE CIVIL WAR, Alexander Gardner. 100 photos taken on field during the Civil War. Famous shots of Manassas, Harper's Ferry, Lincoln, Richmond, slave pens, etc. 244pp. 10⅜ × 8¼.
22731-6 Pa. $9.95

FIVE ACRES AND INDEPENDENCE, Maurice G. Kains. Great back-to-the-land classic explains basics of self-sufficient farming. The one book to get. 95 illustrations. 397pp. 5⅜ × 8½.
20974-1 Pa. $7.95

SONGS OF EASTERN BIRDS, Dr. Donald J. Borror. Songs and calls of 60 species most common to eastern U.S.: warblers, woodpeckers, flycatchers, thrushes, larks, many more in high-quality recording.
Cassette and manual 99912-2 $8.95

A MODERN HERBAL, Margaret Grieve. Much the fullest, most exact, most useful compilation of herbal material. Gigantic alphabetical encyclopedia, from aconite to zedoary, gives botanical information, medical properties, folklore, economic uses, much else. Indispensable to serious reader. 161 illustrations. 888pp. 6½ × 9¼. 2-vol. set. (USO)
Vol. I: 22798-7 Pa. $9.95
Vol. II: 22799-5 Pa. $9.95

HIDDEN TREASURE MAZE BOOK, Dave Phillips. Solve 34 challenging mazes accompanied by heroic tales of adventure. Evil dragons, people-eating plants, bloodthirsty giants, many more dangerous adversaries lurk at every twist and turn. 34 mazes, stories, solutions. 48pp. 8¼ × 11.
24566-7 Pa. $2.95

LETTERS OF W. A. MOZART, Wolfgang A. Mozart. Remarkable letters show bawdy wit, humor, imagination, musical insights, contemporary musical world; includes some letters from Leopold Mozart. 276pp. 5⅜ × 8½.
22859-2 Pa. $7.95

BASIC PRINCIPLES OF CLASSICAL BALLET, Agrippina Vaganova. Great Russian theoretician, teacher explains methods for teaching classical ballet. 118 illustrations. 175pp. 5⅜ × 8½.
22036-2 Pa. $4.95

THE JUMPING FROG, Mark Twain. Revenge edition. The original story of The Celebrated Jumping Frog of Calaveras County, a hapless French translation, and Twain's hilarious "retranslation" from the French. 12 illustrations. 66pp. 5⅜ × 8½.
22686-7 Pa. $3.95

BEST REMEMBERED POEMS, Martin Gardner (ed.). The 126 poems in this superb collection of 19th- and 20th-century British and American verse range from Shelley's "To a Skylark" to the impassioned "Renascence" of Edna St. Vincent Millay and to Edward Lear's whimsical "The Owl and the Pussycat." 224pp. 5⅜ × 8½.
27165-X Pa. $4.95

COMPLETE SONNETS, William Shakespeare. Over 150 exquisite poems deal with love, friendship, the tyranny of time, beauty's evanescence, death and other themes in language of remarkable power, precision and beauty. Glossary of archaic terms. 80pp. 5⁵⁄₁₆ × 8¼.
26686-9 Pa. $1.00

BODIES IN A BOOKSHOP, R. T. Campbell. Challenging mystery of blackmail and murder with ingenious plot and superbly drawn characters. In the best tradition of British suspense fiction. 192pp. 5⅜ × 8½.
24720-1 Pa. $5.95

THE WIT AND HUMOR OF OSCAR WILDE, Alvin Redman (ed.). More than 1,000 ripostes, paradoxes, wisecracks: Work is the curse of the drinking classes; I can resist everything except temptation; etc. 258pp. 5⅜ × 8½. 20602-5 Pa. $5.95

SHAKESPEARE LEXICON AND QUOTATION DICTIONARY, Alexander Schmidt. Full definitions, locations, shades of meaning in every word in plays and poems. More than 50,000 exact quotations. 1,485pp. 6½ × 9¼. 2-vol. set.
Vol. I: 22726-X Pa. $16.95
Vol. 2: 22727-8 Pa. $15.95

SELECTED POEMS, Emily Dickinson. Over 100 best-known, best-loved poems by one of America's foremost poets, reprinted from authoritative early editions. No comparable edition at this price. Index of first lines. 64pp. 5³⁄₁₆ × 8¼.
26466-1 Pa. $1.00

CELEBRATED CASES OF JUDGE DEE (DEE GOONG AN), translated by Robert van Gulik. Authentic 18th-century Chinese detective novel; Dee and associates solve three interlocked cases. Led to van Gulik's own stories with same characters. Extensive introduction. 9 illustrations. 237pp. 5⅜ × 8½.
23337-5 Pa. $6.95

THE MALLEUS MALEFICARUM OF KRAMER AND SPRENGER, translated by Montague Summers. Full text of most important witchhunter's "bible," used by both Catholics and Protestants. 278pp. 6⅝ × 10. 22802-9 Pa. $11.95

SPANISH STORIES/CUENTOS ESPAÑOLES: A Dual-Language Book, Angel Flores (ed.). Unique format offers 13 great stories in Spanish by Cervantes, Borges, others. Faithful English translations on facing pages. 352pp. 5⅜ × 8½.
25399-6 Pa. $8.95

THE CHICAGO WORLD'S FAIR OF 1893: A Photographic Record, Stanley Appelbaum (ed.). 128 rare photos show 200 buildings, Beaux-Arts architecture, Midway, original Ferris Wheel, Edison's kinetoscope, more. Architectural emphasis; full text. 116pp. 8¼ × 11. 23990-X Pa. $9.95

OLD QUEENS, N.Y., IN EARLY PHOTOGRAPHS, Vincent F. Seyfried and William Asadorian. Over 160 rare photographs of Maspeth, Jamaica, Jackson Heights, and other areas. Vintage views of DeWitt Clinton mansion, 1939 World's Fair and more. Captions. 192pp. 8⅞ × 11. 26358-4 Pa. $12.95

CAPTURED BY THE INDIANS: 15 Firsthand Accounts, 1750–1870, Frederick Drimmer. Astounding true historical accounts of grisly torture, bloody conflicts, relentless pursuits, miraculous escapes and more, by people who lived to tell the tale. 384pp. 5⅜ × 8½. 24901-8 Pa. $8.95

THE WORLD'S GREAT SPEECHES, Lewis Copeland and Lawrence W. Lamm (eds.). Vast collection of 278 speeches of Greeks to 1970. Powerful and effective models; unique look at history. 842pp. 5⅜ × 8½. 20468-5 Pa. $14.95

THE BOOK OF THE SWORD, Sir Richard F. Burton. Great Victorian scholar/adventurer's eloquent, erudite history of the "queen of weapons"—from prehistory to early Roman Empire. Evolution and development of early swords, variations (sabre, broadsword, cutlass, scimitar, etc.), much more. 336pp. 6⅛ × 9¼. 25434-8 Pa. $8.95

AUTOBIOGRAPHY: The Story of My Experiments with Truth, Mohandas K. Gandhi. Boyhood, legal studies, purification, the growth of the Satyagraha (nonviolent protest) movement. Critical, inspiring work of the man responsible for the freedom of India. 480pp. 5⅜ × 8½. (USO) 24593-4 Pa. $8.95

CELTIC MYTHS AND LEGENDS, T. W. Rolleston. Masterful retelling of Irish and Welsh stories and tales. Cuchulain, King Arthur, Deirdre, the Grail, many more. First paperback edition. 58 full-page illustrations. 512pp. 5⅜ × 8½.
26507-2 Pa. $9.95

THE PRINCIPLES OF PSYCHOLOGY, William James. Famous long course complete, unabridged. Stream of thought, time perception, memory, experimental methods; great work decades ahead of its time. 94 figures. 1,391pp. 5⅜ × 8½. 2-vol. set.
Vol. I: 20381-6 Pa. $12.95
Vol. II: 20382-4 Pa. $12.95

THE WORLD AS WILL AND REPRESENTATION, Arthur Schopenhauer. Definitive English translation of Schopenhauer's life work, correcting more than 1,000 errors, omissions in earlier translations. Translated by E. F. J. Payne. Total of 1,269pp. 5⅜ × 8½. 2-vol. set. Vol. 1: 21761-2 Pa. $11.95
Vol. 2: 21762-0 Pa. $11.95

MAGIC AND MYSTERY IN TIBET, Madame Alexandra David-Neel. Experiences among lamas, magicians, sages, sorcerers, Bonpa wizards. A true psychic discovery. 32 illustrations. 321pp. 5⅜ × 8½. (USO) 22682-4 Pa. $8.95

THE EGYPTIAN BOOK OF THE DEAD, E. A. Wallis Budge. Complete reproduction of Ani's papyrus, finest ever found. Full hieroglyphic text, interlinear transliteration, word-for-word translation, smooth translation. 533pp. 6½ × 9¼.
21866-X Pa. $9.95

MATHEMATICS FOR THE NONMATHEMATICIAN, Morris Kline. Detailed, college-level treatment of mathematics in cultural and historical context, with numerous exercises. Recommended Reading Lists. Tables. Numerous figures. 641pp. 5⅜ × 8½. 24823-2 Pa. $11.95

THEORY OF WING SECTIONS: Including a Summary of Airfoil Data, Ira H. Abbott and A. E. von Doenhoff. Concise compilation of subsonic aerodynamic characteristics of NACA wing sections, plus description of theory. 350pp. of tables. 693pp. 5⅜ × 8½. 60586-8 Pa. $14.95

THE RIME OF THE ANCIENT MARINER, Gustave Doré, S. T. Coleridge. Doré's finest work; 34 plates capture moods, subtleties of poem. Flawless full-size reproductions printed on facing pages with authoritative text of poem. "Beautiful. Simply beautiful."—*Publisher's Weekly.* 77pp. 9¼ × 12. 22305-1 Pa. $6.95

NORTH AMERICAN INDIAN DESIGNS FOR ARTISTS AND CRAFTS-PEOPLE, Eva Wilson. Over 360 authentic copyright-free designs adapted from Navajo blankets, Hopi pottery, Sioux buffalo hides, more. Geometrics, symbolic figures, plant and animal motifs, etc. 128pp. 8⅜ × 11. (EUK) 25341-4 Pa. $7.95

SCULPTURE: Principles and Practice, Louis Slobodkin. Step-by-step approach to clay, plaster, metals, stone; classical and modern. 253 drawings, photos. 255pp. 8⅛ × 11. 22960-2 Pa. $10.95